I0748421

PRIVATE ENCOUNTERS IN THE PUBLIC WORLD

Philip Ayres

Connor Court Publishing

Published in 2019 by Connor Court Publishing Pty Ltd

ISBN 9781925826548

Connor Court Publishing Pty Ltd
PO Box 7257
Redland Bay QLD 4165
sales@connorcourt.com
www.connorcourtpublishing.com.au

Printed in Australia

Front Cover Image: Antonin Scalia with the author, Cinema Point, Victoria - *Author collection*

Front Cover Design: Maria Giordano

CONTENTS

For Claudio and Maria-Isabel

Illustrations

Preface

The personal encounters described in this book, most of which were political in some way, stretched from 1967 to the present and were the products of friendship, research, happenstance, curiosity or calculated risk. Each account is a biographical or historical vignette and embodies an element of travel. The travel and settings in each case were important because they coloured the encounters and infused the memories. The time I spent in 1967 with an ascendant Soviet leader is explicable only in the context of a miniscule world of fellow travellers connected to me by family and into whose company I occasionally drifted. The correspondence with Diana Mosley was triggered by my work at Chatsworth House—in no other circumstance would the idea have occurred to me. Context is not everything in this book but it's indispensable.

The chapters are not logically sequential or for the most part connected by anything aside from me. There's no theme running through them and I've tried to avoid imposing moral judgments or even thinking in moral terms. The point of view is as judgmental as a tape recorder. If there's an attitude it's open-minded, sceptical and a shade cynical, proceeding from a working assumption that much of what we've read or been taught is at least partly false, often entirely false. There's no animus here against surviving adherents of failed ideologies or desire to convert them. They're taken as found: a charismatic Jamaican socialist whose policies had disastrous consequences and split his island into warring halves, an African president-for-life of Christian conviction who believed that all power is based in violence (arguably true), another next door with his own system of things, a Somali general in an anarchic world of his own making, an Ulster firebrand tamed by time and fatal prognosis, Afghan jihadists funded by an America whose culture they hate, Iranian revolutionaries and various other stand-outs in this panorama of personalities. Even the more regular types have their off-centre aspects that I was well aware of when I was with them: Gerald Ford, pacifist co-founder of the America First Committee (1940), Antonin Scalia, hunter of black bear.

Two or three of the characters rank as political extremists, at least in the view of their enemies, and perhaps there's a psychopath in here somewhere, but they were all reasonable and conversable when I was with them, and I can only record what I see and hear, I can't be in another's mind. To give just one example: in the film *Blackhawk Down* (2001) Hollywood turned the Somali General and former Ambassador to India Mohamed Farrah Aidid into a murderous warlord, but the director and producers of that film wouldn't know and were never there (the city in the film is absurdly unlike Mogadishu). I wouldn't know either, but at the negotiation I witnessed he was reasonable, and the people I was with certainly preferred his control over the town of Bardera to its control by the truly murderous General Morgan. Aidid had right from his side. Something similar goes for the group of left-populists I met one-on-one: Robert Mugabe, Michael Manley and Kenneth Kaunda were all subject to varying degrees of condemnation from the West over the years, some of it doubtless earned, but none of them is or was inherently wicked. One mightn't want to live under their regimes, but how far does one trust "the news", who blended it, and who cooked it?

Everything here happened exactly as described. For many of these encounters I had a tape recorder running or a notebook on my lap (the tapes are with me, but copies are accessible at the University of Melbourne Archives). In addition I have a sharp long-term memory not just of facts but associations, so if I say that the Emperor Waltz was playing in the background, it's because it was. I also *occasionally* remember what I was wearing or what I was pouring myself in a particular hotel room or with friends, because that works by association too, and my range of preferred cocktails is small. The only licence I've allowed myself is to use direct speech in some of the situations where I don't have the evidence of a tape or a notebook, but even there it's based on a sharp memory of what was said.

I'm grateful to the people living and dead who were in some way part of these encounters and gave me their time, friendship or co-operation, and to others who helped by reading draft chapters, urging me to put this collection together, commenting on my work, or publishing certain sections in other forms. The debts stretch across half a century and are too numerous to list but include Louise Adler, the late Philip and Elkin Alston, Richard Alston, Ahmad Attari, the late Fred and Jean Ayres, Julian Ayres, Patricia Ayres, Ghairat Baheer, the late Charles Bohner, Joan Bohner, Neil Brown, Anthony Capello, the late Deborah Cavendish Duchess of Devonshire, the late Alexandrs Drīzulis, the late Gerald Ford, the late Malcolm Fraser, Phoebe Fraser, John Gittings, Abdi Haji Gobdon, Brian Groshinsky, Nick Hasluck, Gulbuddin Hekmatyar, Dyson Heydon, the late Liz Jackson, Kenneth Kaunda, the late Sher Keshtiar, Michael Lawriwsky, Louise Manifold, the late Michael Manley, Robin Marks, Stewart McArthur, Lockton Morrissey, the late Diana Lady Mosley, Robert Mugabe, Allan Myers, Eileen Paisley, the late Ian Paisley (Lord Bannside), Rhonda Paisley, Patrick Radcliffe-Gleeson, Christopher Ricks, Maruta Rodan, Nawab Saleem, the late Antonin

Scalia, Edward Seaga, the late Richard Searby, Alan Simpson, the late Sir Ninian Stephen, Valery Lady Stephen, John Stone, Nancy Stone, Claudio and Maria-Isabel Véliz, Denis White, Keith Windschuttle, and Rhodri Wynn-Pope.

I

Hosting the Soviet Enemy

Aleksandrs Drīzulis, Chairman, Supreme Soviet, Latvian SSR . Open-minded and curious, in Adelaide in 1967 he deserted his tour group for more interesting company. He could do that. Photo in the public domain.

He's not famous anywhere most people are likely to be going, but there was a time when he presided over the legislature of a constituent republic of the USSR, the Latvian Soviet Socialist Republic: Aleksandrs Drīzulis, Chairman of the Latvian Supreme Soviet. When I spent a day and evening with him he was already high-up. He was also an eminent

Marxist–Leninist historian and academician who published a lot of scholarly work (in Latvian), some of which, apparently, has continuing value, and he exemplifies the importance of avoiding moral judgments when dealing with people who made their political career in the higher echelons of Soviet power. His father was bumped off with a shot to the back of the head by the NKVD in the basement of the Lubyanka Building in Moscow in 1939, yet the fatherless youth made an eminent career in the Party, so right there we have a challenge: simplify *that*. He spent a couple of days in Adelaide in 1967 and my first wife and I helped him kill half that time, just the three of us.

Suffice to say he didn't come to meet the Latvians of Adelaide, a substantial immigrant community, two or three thousand strong, economically vibrant and politically interesting, almost all of them refugees from Soviet occupation. I'd married into the community in 1965. Latvia, long part of the Russian Empire, was independent between the Wars, but then forcefully incorporated back into the then-Soviet empire in July 1940 under the secret protocols of the Molotov-Ribbentrop Pact. Tens of thousands of its professional, military and bourgeois elite were deported to Siberia by cattle-class rail as class enemies in the days immediately preceding the German invasion of the Soviet Union in June 1941.

The consequence was that the Germans were welcomed as liberators when they drove the Soviets out. Many Latvians joined the two Latvian Legions that formed part of the Waffen SS. When the Red Army pushed back in the second half of 1944, over a hundred thousand Latvians, as well as large numbers of Lithuanians and Estonians, followed in the wake of the retreating German armies or kept ahead of them, either crowding onto German transport ships that took them down the Baltic to Danzig and Stettin, or walking by the two narrow coastal sand spits of East

Prussia to Danzig and then westward, ending up in various displaced persons' camps somewhere west of the zone of Soviet occupation. They were anti-communist from experience.

My politics were non-visceral: Marxism–Leninism was fundamentally flawed, I thought, because it was based on overt class hatred, which necessarily entailed some kind of civil war; because it didn't appear to work very well with its absence of incentive and private initiative (though it did provide universal literacy, free access to health care, ready access to high culture and other benefits); and because it constituted, to whatever extent, a form of social tyranny. However, I felt no dislike for people who had bought into the ideology, or for apparently intelligent people who had grown up within it and accepted it. A young Adelaide friend of ours whom I'll call Robbo belonged to that section of the Communist Party of Australia whose remnants later hived off as the Socialist Party of Australia, which some in the CPA referred to as "the Tankies" because its members, unlike the CPA majority, *liked* the invasion of Czechoslovakia in 1968—these were the last of the Moscow-line holdouts, unreformed, some of them still Stalinists. Times had changed, but not them. They'd be cold before they'd change. Robbo played the banjo and the guitar, as I guess he'd learned to do in the Eureka Youth League. His politics were nothing to me and we had a lot of fun together.

I suppose it was because my first wife and I shared a cool view of politics that we could enjoy our evenings at the home of my favourite uncle and his wife, Fred and Jean Ayres, who had recently moved into the inner suburb of Medindie from their sheep station up near Mount Pleasant, where in earlier times I used to stay on school holidays—he had high-powered express rifles lined up in their cases and he'd let me shoot them. He also had excellent cameras, movie and still, and he drove an Armstrong Siddeley Sapphire he'd bought new at the Royal Adelaide

Show around 1954 or '55. He'd built a number of motorboats over the years and spent a lot of time fishing from them.

Along with all this good gear, he and his wife possessed surprisingly radical opinions, and they made numerous visits to the USSR. He was the first person to inform me, in about 1958 when I was fourteen or so, that we *hadn't* won the Korean War. As it was my favourite uncle who was telling me this, I checked and he was right. In the view of Fred and Jean, the Hungarian uprising of 1956 was initiated by ex-Arrow-Cross types and anti-Semitic gangs—but if we didn't believe that, they couldn't give a damn. In Fred's capacity as a patron and then president of the state's Australia–Soviet Friendship Society he and Jean would entertain visiting Soviet delegations and tour groups, and they regularly invited us along. He was either *on* the Australian Wool Board (chaired by Sir William Gunn) or attached to it in some capacity and had spent months in Kazakhstan or Uzbekistan investigating the wool industry there, possibly with future exports of Australian merinos in mind, though I don't now recall the details.

We met a lot of Russians and others through Fred and Jean, officials and private individuals including Yevgeny Yevtushenko in 1966 at one of their supper parties, when the poet and cautious dissenter spent the best part of half an hour trying to seduce my wife. I was informed by someone at the party that this was habitual with him. His poetry had an inflated moral tone and was embarrassingly rhetorical. Views on its quality vary. The great Anna Akhmatova memorably dismissed him as no better than an average newspaper satirist, though that was before the appearance of his more mature work, which she didn't live to read. His chief promoter and hanger-on in this country was Geoffrey Dutton, sometime member of the Adelaide English Department and of the exclusive Adelaide Club, from which, in a *Louis Égalité* gesture, he loudly resigned. Dutton played the landed-gentry role for all it was worth, a guaranteed drawcard for Soviet guests like Yevtushenko who loved going up to the old Dutton property and its homestead, Anlaby. Meanwhile Dutton was neglecting agricultural economics, to his ruin.

Late-1967 was the fiftieth anniversary of the Glorious October Revolution, and a Soviet tour group materialised to help the Adelaide faithful celebrate the event. We were invited to a supper party in the group's honour, and it was there that we met Aleksandrs Drīzulis ("Drizul" or "Drizuls" in some Russian sources including the *Great Soviet Encyclopedia*), at that time the 47-year-old Deputy Chairman of the Presidium of the Supreme Soviet of the Latvian SSR, with bigger things ahead: Secretary of the Central Committee of the Communist Party of Latvia in 1970, and ultimately Chairman of the Supreme Soviet of the Latvian SSR (29 March 1985–27 July 1989, succeeded by Anatolijs Gorbunovs, who oversaw the restoration of national independence).

Drīzulis was highly surprised to be introduced to a fellow Latvian. He knew full well that the Latvians in Australia were almost without exception his ideological and war-time enemies, so what would one of them be doing at a Soviet-friendly function like this?—most curious. Curiosity got the better of him. We explained that we were related to the hosts and that this was why we were there. In the course of conversation in Latvian, with English tossed my way from time to time, we asked if he'd like us to collect him at his hotel the following morning.

"Well, we're all meeting in the hotel lobby at 9.00 a.m. for an excursion to the Barossa Valley," he told us in Latvian. "But why not? I'll spend the day with *you*." Because of his position in the hierarchy, I suppose he could do what the hell he liked. It's not true that these groups of Soviet tourists were shepherded about under the tightest restraint—only 99 per cent of them were in that category. People like him (or Yevtushenko) could go where they pleased. This was a pleasant surprise because we'd always imagined that the restraint-figure was 100 per cent.

We used to play "Spot the KGB agent" and I suspect we mostly got it right, because often it would have been the tour leader, and we could work that out. On this occasion I decided that the KGB operative was a woman sitting nearby, a brunette aged around twenty-five or perhaps a good thirty, attractive and wearing discreet and carefully-applied makeup, a midnight-blue dress cut to figure, and two very good legs, crossed. Hence I offered to replenish her vodka-and-orange, and having done that I sat and talked with her. She grew up in Odessa, she said, but now lived in Moscow. She told me I should come to the USSR, as if she really meant it. I told her I'd love to, and that if I did, maybe she could facilitate the trip—perhaps I could even go down to Odessa, and if she happened to be there she could show me through the famous opera house. She almost choked on her screwdriver, but proceeded to inventory her handbag and passed me her calling-card—Latin alphabet, not Cyrillic (she carried both). I have to say that having seen and talked with her that night (and had I not been married) I'd have had no compunction about scoring with the KGB, but there wasn't the chance. I didn't tell her we were about to kidnap one of her charges for a day and night or she might have tried to change his mind, or mine.

We pulled up in front of the Grosvenor Hotel on North Terrace (these Soviet tour groups never used the South Australian Hotel—too up-scale and hence "inappropriate") in a white Toyota Corona at around 8.45 a.m. and got out of the car. I remember all this as if it was yesterday. I wasn't tape-recording anything but what I'm putting in quotes is as close as I can make it.

"What if we're watched? What if we're photographed by some ASIO employee?" Maruta wondered.

"We don't give a damn if we *are* watched and photographed", I told her. "Matter of fact I hope they do photograph us! I hope they have a whole volume of photographs of us. Come on!—we do as we please, like always." It was how I felt that morning. They knew about us anyway if they were on the job, they knew these people were at my uncle's the previous night, and they knew we'd turned up at his house, as we often did. "Anyway", I explained, "we can be certain that right now they aren't on the job because it isn't yet nine a.m., and with a job like theirs they're depressed and hung-over."

I'd had some oblique contact with ASIO as a teenager, or more precisely with their cameras. During my Leaving Honours year, and later while at university, with one or two friends I had occasionally visited the People's Bookshop in Hindley Street where Mrs Moss, wife of leading communist Jim Moss, presided. She never said anything, not that I noticed. The atmosphere inside there was conspiratorial, like that of the Verlocs' shop in Joseph Conrad's *The Secret Agent*, except that instead of selling pornography and contraceptives and plotting anarchist outrages, they were selling communist books and magazines. We'd browse the latest numbers of *Peking Review* and *Soviet Union*, which I thought a good magazine in its way. It was always so quiet in there, as if somebody might be listening, and probably they were. Seldom were there more than two or three other customers. Back on the other side of the street, one floor up in a drab nondescript building, behind its street-front windows were the watchers. Once or twice we'd caught a reflection from their camera lenses. Their obviousness, I assumed, was deliberate. They wished to instil in browsers like us a sense of unease, of records being kept. The Cold War was tangible inside that shop. The Communist Party and the Australia–Soviet Friendship Society were comparatively strong in South Australia, as former Attorney General Neil Brown has told me, so of course ASIO was strong there too.

Some of the Soviet crowd were already descending the stairs inside the lobby, and the KGB woman was in the midst of it all, in a well-cut *black* dress this time, at the foot of the stairs diligently checking them off against her list. She noticed me. Then a group of three descended and the one in the middle was Drīzulis. When he saw us he farewelled his two companions and walked across. She noticed but didn't do anything about it, so perhaps he'd explained it to her, or she didn't dare object. I felt for her, with us just taking him away like that, and later I wished I'd had the chance to apologise—she was easily the best-looking Russian woman I'd met, and it affected the way I thought about the Soviet Union.

We left the car where it was and walked up North Terrace to the Art Gallery of South Australia, where we spent an hour or more in the various halls, with particular attention to nineteenth-century Australian landscapes, which we thought would interest him. I explained about Australian impressionism, Roberts, Streeton and McCubbin, the quest to materialise the Australian light and atmosphere. I specifically remember asking him about Soviet art—had it moved much beyond socialist realism? He said words to the effect that there were many current schools and groups, and Soviet aesthetics were not as ideological and prescribed as they had been. That was a good thing, he added, and we might be surprised.

Over coffee at David Jones, where in those days they served excellent chocolate cakes and cappuccinos, he told us a little about his background—I've since learned more. He was born in 1920 in the ancient Russian city of Pskov, just east of the Estonian border, to pro-Soviet Latvian parents. I discovered in recent years that his father, Arvids Drīzulis ("Arvid Drizul" in Russian sources), a Party worker and friend of Nikolai Yezhov, was arrested in Moscow on 15 September 1938 during the anti-Latvian phase of the Great Terror, sentenced to death as an enemy of the people on 26 February 1939 and shot the same day,[1] after being led into one of the execution chambers in the Lubyanka basement—the walls and floors were lined with asphalt as a sound-deadener and the chambers were equipped with taps and gutters for flushing away the blood. The standard procedure was for the condemned to be held facing the wall by a guard on either side while the executioner fired one shot into the base of the skull with a calibre 7.62mm bullet from a Tokarev semi-automatic pistol.[2] Arvids Drīzulis was posthumously rehabilitated on 12 January 1955. I wonder how many of Aleksandrs' friends ever knew all of that.

This tragedy in Aleksandrs' background, and having to deal with it, would be enough to explain the rapport and affinity we sensed in him. In 1942, at the age of 22, just three years after his father's death, he enrolled in the History and Archive Institute in Moscow, and eight years later was admitted as a member of the Communist Party of the Soviet Union (Stalin still had three years left), with what feelings one shouldn't presume to guess, though on his behalf (because he can't tell us) I'll hazard a guess in any case—he saw his father as the victim of lying, ambitious Party enemies and a flawed system, not of an evil ideology. If he were still alive I'd call him at his home in Riga and ask him, and he'd take the call, but he died in 2006. I remember him telling me that through the 1950s, living in Riga, he devoted himself to scholarly historical studies—along the official line, naturally. He published his work in Latvian, not in Russian. In 1963 he became director of the Latvian Institute of History and a high-ranking academician within the social sciences division of the Academy of Sciences of the Latvian

1 "Arvid Drizul", Time Note, 12 April, from the webpage https://nekropole.info, citing documentary sources. Sourced 20 January 2016. See also Nikita Petrov, *Stalin's Loyal Executioner: People's Commissar Nikolai Ezhov, 1885–1940* (Hoover Institution Press Publication), pp. 3-4.

2 Relevant sections of Timothy J. Colton, *Moscow: Governing the Socialist Metropolis* (Harvard University Press, Cambridge, Massachesetts, 1998).

SSR. He talked to us about his historical work because I asked him to, and he could see I took it seriously. A senior academician is more than a common garden-variety propagandist. New facts and hard research are actually required, it's not *all* spin.

Anyone as cognizant as he obviously was about the complexities of Latvian history (key Bolsheviks were Latvian, and Latvian riflemen were the shock-troops of the Bolshevik Revolution) could not, privately, have seen everything in black-and-white, and it was clear he didn't. My wife told him straight-out that she and her family were anti-communist and had followed the Germans out of the country in 1944. Of course he knew that already. All he said was that history had divided us yet here we were together. He never once tried to persuade us that the present Latvian SSR was preferable to the pre-war independent republic (he avoided calling it "the bourgois republic" as he normally would have done), because he knew it would be a waste of breath, and why spoil a nice outing? He was spending the day with us so we felt somewhat honoured, given his position, and it was going to be the evening too because we'd already asked him to join us for dinner at our second-floor Unley Park flat, the kitchen windows of which looked down over leafy Victoria Terrace.

I paid the bill, we strolled back to where we'd left the car and headed for the hills. As we drove through Piccadilly Valley and on towards Lobethal I asked him how he came to enter parliament. He said it was a natural-enough move for an academician like him. I asked about the one-party state and the single-candidate voting paper. He said I mightn't believe him, but his name on that voting paper couldn't be taken for granted by him, and his constituents could and often did press complaints on him. They could make a very big fuss indeed, and the press would be inclined to be on their side. He also told me that many of the candidates in elections were non-party people—yes, there was just the one party, but the party was in a bloc with non-party people (by permission or choice of party people, I assume). I'd never heard of that. I hadn't read J. L. Talmon's *Totalitarian Democracy* very closely, though I'd read some of it. I also asked him why it was that the Soviet Government, if it was so popular, didn't permit a loyal opposition. He had some complicated answer he obviously knew was doublespeak. I told him I sometimes borrowed the magazine *Soviet Union* from my uncle or bought it, and that I'd been impressed by photographs showing Soviet children presenting their class teacher with bunches of flowers on the first day of the school year. "*We* should do that *here*," I told him, "but there's no respect for forms, Aleks. We're embarrassed by overt displays of affection. It just couldn't happen in an Australian school". He seemed surprised that I'd mention *that*, probably thought I was crazy, but fifty years later I can still see the photograph.

We drove by the home of my mother's people and I told him about the German immigration of the 1830s and 40s. Then we took him into the oldest Lutheran church in Australia, St John's *Zum Weinberg Christi* (1843-45) with its pale-blue interior, and pointed out the baptismal font where I was christened, the altar, the highly elevated pulpit, the Cross, talked about the longevity of German religious culture in the valley, and said we presumed his people were Lutherans like most Latvians. Well, why *not* take a prominent Soviet Communist through such an interesting church? And why not assume he had a Lutheran family background and was maybe half-way a believer? I wanted him to think about that. Wandering out into the street, we climbed back into the car and drove to the Oakbank Hotel where we questioned him on his political position over a lunch of steak and chips. He said his post as Deputy Chairman of the Presidium of the Latvian Supreme Soviet followed on from his election the previous year as a member of the Central Committee of the Communist Party of Latvia, but he was more interested in asking us questions, and told us how much he loved the Australian beers just as I was getting up to buy him another.

Back in the city we took him around a few more sights and then drove to our Unley Park flat with its elevated views. After drinks, around 7.00 p.m. we cooked him a light meal followed by sweets and coffee, then dropped him off at the Grosvenor somewhere around 11.00 p.m. He thanked us profusely and invited us to visit him back home.

It would have been interesting to have paid the visit, either in Soviet or independent Latvia, though by the time the country had regained its independence we'd divorced. My first wife visited Latvia in the post-Soviet era but she'd half-forgotten about Aleksandrs and in any case didn't have his address. She might have enjoyed looking him up had it occurred to her. I'd half-forgotten him too—or rather forgotten to remember him. The details had mostly remained intact. What brought him to the front of my mind, and brought so many of the details back, was a mean little article I read on-line, from Stanford University's Hoover Institution website,[3] that mentioned a visit he made to the Institution in late 1967, obviously on the same trip that brought him to Australia. Back home, he reported on the visit in a talk to party activists on 18 April 1968. The text of his talk has "Stratford University" for "Stanford University," possibly a transcription error by a typist or printer but probably Drīzulis's own. He mentions Alexander Kerensky being a guest at the Hoover Institution and calls him a "political corpse." Kerensky, who headed the Russian Provisional Government (February–October 1917), had lived in Australia in the mid-1940s. I don't put much store in the Hoover Institution piece, as they hadn't even discovered the date of

3 "A Soviet Vignette of the Hoover Institution, May 25, 2012", https://hoover.org/news, sourced 13 April 2019.

Arvids Drīzulis's execution (which they called "probable"). Someone at the Hoover Institution was lazy. It wasn't hard for me to find those facts. And it's either a lie or a lazy guess for that same writer to say that "He took an early retirement" on Latvia's regaining its independence—he was already 71 in 1991, so it was a *late* retirement.

There exists a publicly accessible private diary in which he figures, the diary of Anatoly Chernyaev, a Soviet historian who later became principal foreign policy adviser to Mikhail Gorbachev, having previously been with the Central Committee's International Department as senior analyst. Chernyaev donated his diaries to the National Security Archive at George Washington University, which has published some of the volumes in translation. Chernyaev died in Moscow in 2017. In May 1972 he led a three-man official delegation of the Central Committee of the CPSU to Sweden, the other two members being Drīzulis and Mikhail Zimyanin, editor-in-chief of *Pravda.* Their mission was to try to mend relations with the Left Party–Communists (LP–C) of Sweden, who had been highly critical of the CPSU over several years. The delegation got on much better with Prime Minister Olof Palme and his Social Democrats, who treated them with more respect. Aside from official meetings, the delegation went to various entertainments, including the Lido nightclub/cinema: "porno films alternating with live performances", Chernyaev noted. On another occasion they visited a sex shop: "Bought some dildos. Very expensive—half my cash is gone".[4] This tells you all you need to know about the moral tone near the apex of Soviet power in the 1970s. These guys were not ideologues, just regular chaps on a jaunt, as decadent as any Westerner, friends of Brezhnev, himself a reasonable guy, as Gerald Ford told me he found. Glaznost and perestroika were

4 *The Diary of Anatoly S. Chernyaev, 1972, donated by A. S. Chernyaev to the National Security Archive*, translated by Anna Melyakova, edited by Svetlana Savranskaya. The pdf is available at https://nsarchive2.gwu.edu/NSAEBB/NSAEBB379/1972. Sourced 13 April 2019.

already predictable, quietly sleeping in their causes.

In independent Latvia, Drīzulis lived retired and quietly until his death in 2006. No one bothered him, from what I've read. He was at base an academic, not a typical politician. In any case the national mood after 1991 was not vindictive. Post-independence books and articles on Latvian history still frequently cite his research, which had objective value in spite of its Marxist line. His ideology reposes in the graveyard of lost causes—as the Hoover Institution's cheap-shot bullseye has it, "the dustbin of history." I can't say I knew him but it was pleasant being with him. I don't think his country's independence would have depressed him. When he was with us in 1967, at the time of the Prague Spring and the fiftieth anniversary of the October Revolution, there were already strong liberal and even independence-minded currents at work among Riga's young intelligentsia, particularly in the arts.[5] He admitted as much. Times change, and by the time he was Chairman of the Latvian Supreme Soviet, from 1985 to 1989, they were changing fast.

5 "The Aftermath of the Prague Spring and Charter 77 in Latvia/the Baltics," exhibition. http://www.lvarhivs.gov.lv/Praga68/. Sourced 13 April 2019.

2

Gerald Ford at Rancho Mirage

Gerald Ford with Brezhnev, Vladivostok Summit, 24 November 1974. In conversation with the author at Rancho Mirage, Ford contrasted his balanced attitude to the USSR with Malcolm Fraser's unbalanced attitude.

After a sleepless trans-Pacific flight I was finally on my back and staring at the ceiling of a room at the Hacienda Santa Rita, a cheap motel adjacent to Los Angeles Airport and directly under an inbound flight path. Every sixty seconds a plane would scream across, then I'd listen for the roar of its reverse thrust blending into the howl of the next one coming on in. The thermostat was stuck on 74°, the windows were fixed shut, there was no minibar and no service. I had no earplugs, and after 1.00 a.m., when the planes stopped flying in, it was the cheap cologne they use in these places that kept me awake. Rain was at the window and with nothing on TV I turned on the radio, a jazz station that wasn't playing "I'd Rather Have the Blues" but should have been.

They don't *poach* eggs there, so I skipped a greasy breakfast and walked the wet streets till I found a newsagency where I bought the 15 January 1986 *Los Angeles Times* and an issue of *Cycle* for an article about the fastest production bike to that time, the Kawasaki GPz1000RX (159 mph, it said). I preferred Ducatis for their engines and their looks, and I had one at home, a 1975 750 Super Sport, but perhaps it needed a companion. Back in the room I took the address book from the inside pocket of my blazer and called a number in Rancho Mirage. The appointment for tomorrow was still on—"Drive into the compound", she said, "the guards will let you on through". Then I found a specialist rental agency and selected a suitable vehicle.

Later, propped up by the pillows, I read the paper. Donna Reed had just died at 64. I remembered her in *It's a Wonderful Life* and I liked the James Stewart character with the courage to stand on that bridge and contemplate the beckoning river. In Alabama George Wallace was contemplating a record fifth term as Governor. Nuclear tests were down by half. California's wild condors were practically extinct. Some local legislators had failed to ban "all you can drink" contests with liquor prizes for winners, offered by bars to attract patrons. Some police officer in Colorado had just shot his wife's divorce lawyer twice at close range. By the third paragraph I'd concluded that the victim had it coming.

From Los Angeles east to Rancho Mirage is 119 miles on Interstate 10. From East Los Angeles Interchange it's known as the San Bernardino Freeway as far as that city, running through Monterey Park, San Gabriel, Pomona and Claremont before entering Riverside County, where it crosses the San Gorgonio Pass between the San Bernardino Mountains to the north and the San Jacinto Mountains to the south. Some distance further on it passes by Palm Springs, Rancho Mirage and Palm Desert and keeps going all the way to Jacksonville in Florida, where I'd be bound by air the next morning.

Just east of White Water I noticed the wind turbines coming into view up on the left side as I drove through the long and windy Pass. You couldn't miss them, there were hundreds, maybe thousands, installed over the previous years, with many more to come. I'd never seen anything like it, though I understood their scientific function. Their logical function, the President later explained to me, was to make money in the form of subsidies for the people who'd bought ownership in them. The net result was that the State made a substantial loss. To left and right the mountains rose to 10,000 feet.

I stopped off the highway at a drive-in for a drink. Few Australians, to the best of my knowledge, had conducted a face-to-face, one-on-one interview with an American President or ex-President in his own home. Gerald Ford had agreed to it as a friend of Malcolm Fraser, about whom I was carrying out far-flung inquiries in odd places. I admired much of what I'd gleaned about Ford, thirty-eighth President of the United States (1974–1977), a moderate Republican whose political roots lay deep in the American isolationist tradition, though the Second World War converted him to a constructive form of internationalism. He never created or exacerbated an international conflict. I admired his pardoning of Richard Nixon because the alternative would have been too reminiscent of countries like Pakistan where they put ex-Presidents on trial and hang them. When Ford was House Minority Leader, Lyndon Johnson said of him "Jerry Ford's so dumb he can't fart and chew gum at the same time" (the press changed it to "walk and chew gum"), and on another occasion quipped that Ford had spent too much time playing football without a helmet. These comments were prompted by Ford's opposition to Johnson's policies in Vietnam where, as he liked to point out, there was no clearly-conceived end-game. Although he slipped and stumbled once or twice during his Presidency, Ford had been a star football player in his college days so he couldn't have been inherently clumsy. He had a reputation for honesty and kindliness.

Ford's parents split up two weeks after his birth (14 July 1913) when his father walked out. This trumps Sir Ninian Stephen, whose father didn't walk out until *three* weeks after his birth. Disaster in these instances was Providence because to an apparently cruel blow of fate all that followed was fortunately owed. With his mother, Ford moved to Michigan, growing up in Grand Rapids. Through the early 1930s he was at the University of Michigan, working nights to put himself through. In 1938 he was accepted into the Yale University Law School from which he graduated LL.B. in 1941. Meanwhile he'd been working as part of Wendell Wilkie's 1940 Republican Presidential campaign.

On 4 September 1940 Gerald Ford was one of the four foundation signatories to a petition designed to enforce the Roosevelt Administration's 1939 Neutrality Act. Along with fellow Yale law students Sargent Shriver (who later married John F. Kennedy's sister Eunice, served in the Kennedy and Johnson Administrations, and ran for Vice-President in the 1972 campaign of George McGovern), Potter Stewart (later on the Supreme Court), and R. Douglas Stuart Jr (Quaker Oats heir), Gerald Ford founded the America First Committee which at its peak had close to a million paid-up members. This was the pre-eminent anti-interventionist, anti-war movement in America and it enjoyed wide support far beyond its impressive membership size. Charles Lindbergh was their chief spokesman; other prominent supporters, who came from both right and left, included the novelist Sinclair Lewis, the poet

E. E. Cummings, Gore Vidal and Walt Disney. When Donald Trump advocates "America First" the historic resonance is intended: keep out of other people's wars if at all possible.

When the bombing of Pearl Harbor forced FDR's declaration of war on Japan, followed by Germany's declaration of war on the United States, Ford enlisted in the Navy and saw action in the Western Pacific on board the light aircraft carrier USS *Monterey* (CVL-26). On 18-19 December 1944 this ship along with others in the Third Fleet under Admiral Halsey was hit by a typhoon that sank three destroyers and caused a fire on board the *Monterey* when aircraft tore free from their cables and slid about, colliding with one another. As the carrier tossed in the storm, Ford lost his footing, slid towards the edge of the deck and was saved only by a two-inch-high perimeter ridge, enough to stop his slide.

He entered Congress in 1949 and sat in the House of Representatives for 25 years, becoming its Minority Leader at the beginning of 1965. When Spiro Agnew resigned as Vice-President in 1973 Nixon chose Ford to replace him, and when Nixon resigned on 9 August 1974 Ford succeeded him, the only man ever to have become President without having been elected to either that office or the Vice-Presidency. A month later he granted Nixon a pardon, and in the view of most observers time has vindicated that action. Ford also opened the way to pardons for draft dodgers who had fled abroad during the Vietnam War, and he granted a full pardon to Tokyo Rose (Iva Toguri D'Aquino), whose post-war conviction for treason had been shown to be partly based on false evidence. Though over two-thirds of the House was Democratic and opposed to some of his key foreign policy measures, he successfully pushed ahead with a balanced Middle East policy that produced the Sinai Interim Agreement.

In 1948, during his first run for the House, Ford married Elizabeth Bloomer Warren, divorcée, former model and professional dancer, and their relations remained close until his death. She told a reporter that the one question no newspaperman had ever asked her was "How often do you have sex?" and that the answer would have been "As often as possible". One of the impressive things about her was how she turned her problems around, in the process helping others face the same issues—she enormously increased awareness of breast cancer in the United States following her mastectomy, and part of her way of dealing with her alcoholism and drug dependency was to establish the Betty Ford Clinic in Rancho Mirage to treat people for substance abuse. She campaigned for the Equal Rights Amendment and publicly backed a range of women's issues from within the Republican White House, her liberal attitudes (which her husband shared) upsetting many of the Party's social conservatives. At the time of my visit she was working on an account of her own treatment, which was published in 1987.

From the Pass it's a long downhill run into the Coachella Valley, past Palm Springs, and then you take an exit right to Rancho Mirage. Strange name. All this area was desert and sand up to the 1930s. What would later become a desirable resort grew out of the Annenberg or Sunnylands Estate after World War II when the place was known as "the eleven-mile spot" and attracted the kind of names that drew ever-increasing numbers: Bob Hope, Frank Sinatra, Fred Astaire, Ginger Rogers. These and other prominent personalities made their homes out here, or rather one of their homes, partly to escape the smog of Los Angeles on weekends. For some reason Clark Gable and Jean Harlow liked the place before it had become so much as a village. Summers are hot, up to 120° F, but this was winter so it was mildly warm. There were around 8,000 inhabitants when I was there in 1986. The Cahuilla Indians had lived out here in the open desert for hundreds of years, and one of the attractions for them was the hot springs. The Spanish called it *Agua Caliente.*

After turning off I-10 I made for the Thunderbird Country Club, the first 18-hole golf course in the Coachella Valley (1951), where the thirteenth hole was overlooked by the 1970s single-storey, ranch-style Ford house at 40471 Sand Dune Road, modest by Presidential standards (just 63 squares) and in that respect reflecting the Fords themselves. They'd moved here following his defeat in the 1976 election, but he'd played golf in Rancho Mirage since the 1960s. I turned off the street and swung into the compound, got out and was shown into his office where we shook hands. He invited me to sit down beside his desk.

He was wearing an open-necked shirt under his jacket, and corduroy trousers, if I rightly recall. Resuming his seat behind the desk, he leaned back and in the process swung his feet up and onto it.

"Excuse me having my feet up here, Philip, but I have arthritic knees", he explained, "and if I don't give them a rest they don't operate." He told me he'd been playing golf with Bob Hope, and that a few days later he'd be playing in the pro-am section of the Bob Hope Classic, so he had to go easy on his knees—too many swings had almost done for them.

I'd envisaged that my conversation with Ford (which is all on tape) would revolve around his impressions of Malcolm Fraser's foreign policy, but it quickly developed into a far more interesting exposition of Ford's own policies on China and the Soviet Union combined with polite criticism of Fraser's attitudes. In the process I learned something about the difference between global and merely regional responsibility. A kind of moral animus against the Soviet Union was something Fraser could afford to indulge, within his responsibility-light geopolitical thinking (he was free of any moral bent against China, on the other hand). To Ford, that kind of animus was counter-productive, just a hindrance to realistic agreements. *Realpolitik* was the only credible approach to great-power relations in a world packed with the obscenity of nuclear weapons—*realpolitik à la* Henry Kissinger, whom Nixon had had the brains to choose as his chief foreign-policy adviser, and whom Ford had had the sense to keep on. Later on Fraser would himself become increasingly cold-blooded on international issues.

So we didn't spend much time on the November 1975 dismissal from office of Prime Minister Gough Whitlam and its consequences. "My recollection", Ford told me, "is that we were favourably inclined, not that we had *bad* relations with the Whitlam Government, but our feeling was that the economic policies, the defence policies, the foreign policy of the new government would be more compatible with my Administration in Washington."

I mentioned Fraser's view that the Soviets had never been serious about *détente*, and his strong belief, particularly during the Carter years, that the West should have been building up its force levels in the face of increasing Soviet levels.

It was more complicated than that, Ford told me, though he agreed with the criticism of Carter's policy. The USSR *had* been serious about *détente* during Nixon's and Ford's Administrations and real progress could have been achieved had he been given a second term, he insisted.

"Let me go back a bit", he added. "When Nixon was President that was sort of a *peak* of *détente*. We signed a number of agreements with the Soviet Union that included SALT I [Strategic Arms Limitation Talks I] and an anti-[killer]-satellite program. Then of course the problem expanded with the deterioration of the situation in Vietnam and allegations that the Soviet Union was in violation of SALT I, etcetera, and there was growing unrest in the United States as to our relations with the Soviet Union—the more conservative element in the United

States in particular. In my Administration I finally stopped using the word "*détente*". I thought it was misunderstood. As a word it didn't *mean* anything to the vast majority of the American people.

"So I stopped using it even though I personally believed that the United States and the Soviet Union ought to have a continuous dialogue with the full recognition that there are issues which are more or less unsolvable but there are other issues on a global or regional level where there can be progress made, and that you ought to seek, through dialogue, to exploit any breakthroughs that might take place. And I happen to believe that my Administration could have achieved a SALT II agreement with the Soviet Union following my Vladivostok negotiations with Brezhnev if I had been elected."

This was in reference to their talks of November 1974, detailed in Ford's book *A Time to Heal* (Harper Row, New York, 1979). The first Strategic Arms Limitation Agreement, reached in May 1972, was due to expire in 1977, and the Vladivostok talks were intended to secure a more permanent and wide-ranging accord—"to put a cap on the arms race and further the chances for a lasting peace", as Ford put it (p. 214). Ford and Brezhnev struck up a particularly warm relationship and an agreement on the most substantial issue was indeed reached: 2400 ballistic missiles for each country, with no more than 1320 on each side MIRVed—topped with multiple independently-targetable re-entry vehicles (warheads); this meant the USSR would reduce its missiles by around 300. Some issues remained unresolved, including the B1 bomber then in development and production of the Trident submarine.

"We had achieved about a 95-per-cent agreement at Vladivostok", Ford told me, "and if I had been elected, through negotiations with the Soviet Union and through dialogue we could have accomplished a SALT II agreement that Congress would have ratified in 1977. Now, when Mr

Carter came in he abandoned the negotiating posture that I had taken on the SALT II and threw a new proposal to the Soviet Union which was totally different, and when you shift gears on the Soviets 180 degrees it upsets them, they don't understand it. That really created a roadblock in Soviet–United States relations."

So in Ford's view the Soviet Union was not responsible in this connection, it was the Carter Administration that had derailed the train. Ford's perspective, informed by his own first-hand negotiating experience and subsequent close observation of things, was diametrically opposed to Fraser's anti-Soviet, Cold-War reflexes on the matter.

"Well, then the Carter Administration", he continued, "after seeing the mistake they'd made, went back to almost the proposal that I had suggested, but unfortunately in the meantime they had cut back on certain strategic weapons, cancelled the B1 bomber, and so they were negotiating more or less the same deal I tried to promote but had cut back our military capabilities.

"Now Malcolm, I guess, was upset with, or certainly non-supportive of *détente* as he understood it. I never really knew whether he objected to it on the surface or really objected to the process. The process of negotiation I think is sound, and if I were President today I would still pursue the process of trying to resolve regional or global problems with the Soviet Union. The difference is I would insist on having a fully adequate military capability in case we weren't able to make progress. That's the distinction between Carter and Ford. We insisted that our military capability be sufficient to meet any contingency while at the same time you're proceeding with diplomatic initiatives."

I raised another point of geopolitical interest, again one where Ford's views turned out to be very different from Fraser's, that emerged out of the first overseas trip Fraser made as Prime Minister, to the People's

Republic of China in mid-1976, shortly before he visited the United States for discussions with Ford's Administration. In China Fraser had been regaled in a manner Whitlam never had been, because Fraser made no secret of his animosity towards the Soviet Union (Whitlam, by contrast, had gone so far in his positive approach to the USSR as to formally recognise its 1940 annexation of the Baltic States). In China Fraser was outspokenly supportive of the Chinese in their arguments with Moscow, was shown around strategic military installations and witnessed a demonstration of firepower put on by the Peking Military Garrison's division outside the capital. He was reported to be toying with the idea of a four-power agreement ("pact", the newspapers called it), including some military element, which would tie together the United States, Japan, China and Australia.

I asked Ford whether Fraser had ever discussed this idea with him, and what he thought of it. Did he think it originated as a Chinese idea they wanted Fraser to raise in Washington, or was it just Fraser's idea?

"I do not feel that the Chinese were using Malcolm", Ford replied. "I say that because we—my Administration—had developed very good relations with the Deng Xiaoping regime in China. When I visited Deng Xiaoping in 1975 I was greatly impressed with him. Almost immediately thereafter he was dumped, put out to pasture so to speak, but he came back, and I was and still am a great admirer of Deng Xiaoping. I think he's done a fantastic job with China. And our relations *vis-à-vis* China at that time were excellent. We agreed that we didn't *have* to have a military alliance, it was better just to have excellent relations without becoming too closely tied in a military sense. If China and the United States had become that closely tied it might, in a strange way, have been counter-productive in both countries' dealings with the Soviet Union. It's better for us both to have similar views *vis-à-vis* the Soviet Union but not necessarily to be tied together in the *expression* of those views or the execution of those views.

"So we understood what Malcolm was trying to promote, but from our point of view a four-power arrangement, number one, would have been most difficult to achieve bearing in mind the Chinese attitudes, bearing in mind the military problems that exist in Japan, with their limitation of one per cent of GNP on what they can expend on the army, navy and air force etcetera, I don't think that would ever have been practical to achieve; but secondly, I'm not sure it would have been in the best interests in carrying out what we believed was a good relationship with China on the one hand and a good relationship with the Soviet Union on the other."

We discussed a wide range of other issues including trade negotiations, but the discussion on strategic issues was the most revealing, and what it revealed particularly was the set of problems inherent in the attitudes being articulated by Fraser.

Ford liked Fraser and knew him well through the meetings of the American Enterprise Institute World Forum that Ford established in 1982 that brought together, at Vail in Colorado, a range of former and current world leaders and prominent business figures for discussions on political and economic issues. Ford hosted these meetings and Fraser attended a number of them, each one lasting a week or so. "We enjoy his company", Ford told me. "We have a lot of things in common. I've heard some people say at the World Forum that he talks a little too long. He gets started on something and he'll take ten minutes for what he could say in five. Now I've heard some of the people say that. I think that's unfortunately a habit that too many politicians have. But he's knowledgeable, he's articulate, he'll fight hard on a point. He's very concerned about the world monetary system, the free market in currencies etcetera. He has a sound view on world trade, strong views on GATT. Good broad perspectives."

At the time, Fraser was a member of an Eminent Persons' Group trying to bring the African National Congress and other outlawed opposition forces in South Africa into a dialogue with the Government. Ford disagreed with Fraser's hard-line support of international sanctions. "Yes, he told me he was going to be spending some time on that project. My only comment on South Africa would be, and I say it sadly, you have an immovable object faced with a train that's coming down the track. Immovable object, irresistible force. No solution. It's sad. I think we're all opposed to Apartheid, I am, but I honestly don't see how total divestiture of American interests in South Africa is going to help one black person get a better education, a better house and a better job. We've got to find some way to convince the Government there to find a better solution than the existing circumstances. I'm not an expert, but I don't see how sanctions are producing affirmative results."

In this instance Ford's perspective proved flawed, as it turned out to be external pressure more than anything else that forced the immoveable object to move.

I drove back to the motel by the way I'd come. That evening, on a midnight flight to Jacksonville, I played back through my earphones the hour-long interview I'd taped, thinking how Ford kept things in perspective, and how important that has to be in such an office. He'd remained true to the best within the early heritage of his political life, and back in 1986 it would not have surprised me to know that eighteen years into the future he would criticise George W. Bush's invasion of Iraq, an action heavily influenced by neo-conservative ideologues, some with theoretical roots in Trotsky of all people, who thought the world could be remade in America's image. "Well, I can understand the theory of wanting to free people", Ford would say in 2004 in reference to a statement by Bush that the United States had a "duty to free people". But it was another matter entirely, in Ford's view, "whether you can detach that from obligation number one, of what's in our national interest. And I just don't think we should go hellfire damnation around the globe 'freeing people' unless it is directly related to our national security." (*Washington Post*, 28 December 2006, embargoed interview of 2004 reported by Bob Woodward following Ford's death).

Today Ford's long-held anti-interventionist views find their counterparts within the Trump Administration's America First line and among the voters who strongly support it, and on the Democratic side in the foreign policy views of Bernie Sanders, even more anti-interventionist and highly critical of what Eisenhower identified scathingly as "the military–industrial complex". There are still predictable pressures in an interventionist direction from post-dated neo-conservative elements within one or two of the older think tanks, and from rogue elements inside the Deep State, but domestic priority has such wide support now on both sides of the party divide that it's hard to see it changing, especially given the size of the national debt. Ford, with two or three others, *created* the concept and slogan America First.

3

Manley, Kaunda, Mugabe

Michael Manley with Fidel Castro, Montego Bay, Jamaica, 1977. In conversation with the author in Kingston, Manley credited his friendship with Castro for Cuba's non-interference in the 1979 Zimbabwe process.

Margaret Thatcher's attempt to secure Commonwealth recognition of the moderate, black-and-white, Abel Muzorewa–Ian Smith government in Zimbabwe was derailed at the Commonwealth Heads of Government Meeting in Lusaka (1–7 August 1979), and Thatcher was compelled to agree to a process of negotiations leading to elections that predictably gave power to Robert Mugabe and his party. In 1986 I set out to explore the background to her defeat at Lusaka and Mugabe's ascension to power, and to build that into the Fraser biography then in train. I knew what Fraser had told me of his role behind the scenes, but I didn't have the other perspectives required to understand the engineering. That meant consulting the relevant heads of state: Michael Manley of Jamaica, Julius Nyerere of Tanzania, Kenneth Kaunda of Zambia, and the ultimate recipient of their efforts, Robert Mugabe. I also met with Thatcher's Foreign Secretary Lord Carrington, Commonwealth Secretary-General Shridath (Sonny) Ramphal, but not Thatcher herself, who intensely disliked Fraser—her private secretary told me straight-out, "No way she'll see you".

As I was in the Americas, I decided to begin in Jamaica, and it was there that Michael Manley explained the roles of significant unseen players about whose parts in the game I knew nothing: President Jimmy Carter, his Ambassador to the United Nations Andrew Young, and Fidel Castro. I recorded the interview, as I did the others. Most of the details about Carter, all the details on Nyerere's and Young's influence on Carter's perception of the Rhodesian issue, and reflections on Castro's position were not built into the biography because they were only tangentially connected with the central Fraser–Manley–Nyerere–Kaunda axis on which I was focused. I now believe the Carter-, Young-, Castro-related material has at least as much historical and geopolitical importance as the material relating to Fraser's role.

I'd already arrived at one remove from Carter when I got to Jamaica because I'd stayed a few days on Sea Island, Georgia, with Philip Alston and his wife Elkin, close friends of the Carters. Alston had chaired the Committee for Jimmy Carter in 1976, the year Carter was elected President, and subsequently Carter had appointed him Ambassador to Australia. I told them I was going down to Jamaica to see Manley, whose personal relations with Carter had been warm, but they knew little about Manley except that he was a pal of Castro's. From Sea Island I drove to Jacksonville, flew to Miami and caught another plane south across Cuba for the Island in the Sun to meet with the past-and-future socialist Prime Minister of Jamaica at his Kingston home on a sunny Friday, 24

January 1986. Perhaps because he had few responsibilities in opposition, Michael Manley gave me well over an hour of his time.

Born in 1924 into the old Jamaican elite, more white than black, radically-left politically (like his father Norman Washington Manley, brilliant lawyer and Rhodes Scholar, co-founder in 1938 of the People's National Party or PNP), Michael Manley stood tall and cut a slim figure in his Kariba suit, worn without a shirt (or the jacket *was* the shirt). He was exciting to be around, to be with—whatever it was that he radiated, part of it, he always said, was love, a word he overused. Educated in the best Jamaican schools and then at McGill University in Montreal, he trained on Hurricanes as a pilot officer with the Royal Canadian Air Force in the later stages of the Second World War and subsequently studied at the London School of Economics under Harold Laski. Early influences on Manley's thinking included Garveyism, the black-nationalist movement (predecessor of the Black Power movement and Nation of Islam), founded by the Jamaican Marcus Garvey.

Alternately sitting down and pacing the big living room, he described his role in the anti-Thatcher conspiracy in great detail. It was intriguing to watch him. Manley epitomised cool in his looks and language and had a restless energy that was both kinetic and intellectual. Loved by one half of the nation and hated by the other, he and his populist People's National Party had transformed Jamaica from 1972 to 1980 by introducing free education for all, a minimum wage, equal pay for women, redistribution of landed estates, and accelerated construction of houses and hospitals, all financed by greatly increased taxes on private corporations, on the rich and the middle class. Side effects were severe and included record inflation and unemployment. Foreign investment dried up and the middle class emigrated in droves. Elections in 1976 and 1980 were vitiated by deadly shoot-outs in the streets between members of the PNP and Edward Seaga's Jamaican Labour Party—hundreds were gunned down. Under President Gerald Ford and his Secretary of State Henry Kissinger, Washington predictably contrived to destabilise things further as Manley developed ever-closer ties with Cuba. Having failed to get Manley to come to see him in Washington, Kissinger had to fly down to Kingston to demand that Manley condemn Cuba's sending of troops to assist Angola's government in battling Jonas Savimbi's rebel UNITA forces, who were backed by South Africa and to some extent the United States. Manley refused point-blank.

"We have that friendship with Cuba as part of a world alliance of Third World nations that are fighting for justice for poor people in the world," he told one crowd of supporters. "We intend to walk through the world on our feet and not on our knees," he told another.

The interview got underway and a notebook would have been useless because Manley was speaking quickly, walking about, sometimes away from me, so that a few words and phrases on the tape are blurred in playback. One of the phrases he used a lot was "the Muzorewa betrayal". By this he meant Rhodesia's Internal Settlement of 1978 between Ian Smith and Bishop Abel Muzorewa. The elections of April 1979, at which there was one electoral roll for whites (20 seats), another for every adult in the country (72 seats), and eight non-constituency seats, also for whites, had resulted in a moderate black-majority government under Muzorewa and his United African National Congress (UANC) for a new "Zimbabwe–Rhodesia", backed by Smith and his Rhodesian Front. It was a "some-men-one-vote, other-men-two-votes" system. Neither the Zimbabwe African National Union–Patriotic Front (ZANU–PF) led by Robert Mugabe, nor the Zimbabwe African People's Union (ZAPU) led by Joshua Nkomo, had been allowed to run, because they had not agreed to cease hostilities. The results had been condemned by the United Nations Security Council as unrepresentative of the popular will, with the United States, Britain, France, Canada and West Germany abstaining.

Britain's abstention signalled its willingness to recognise the new government, and the abstention of the United States had pointed in the same direction, one promptly reversed, as Manley reminded me.

"There had been a very important development", he went on, "when the Senate of the United States voted to lift sanctions because of the Muzorewa agreement, and Carter, undoubtedly prompted by Andy Young, vetoed it, which is an often-forgotten step in the chain of events that led to the eventual outcome." Andrew Young, Carter's Ambassador to the United Nations, with whom Michael Manley had enjoyed a close friendship for years, backed Mugabe and Nkomo.

Manley then told me something I've never seen mentioned and found highly interesting: how his friend Andrew Young's influence on Carter in this respect had been facilitated by Tanzania's Julius Nyerere.

"You know, the thing that really planted an understanding of Zimbabwe in Carter's mind was Nyerere, who went all the way to Washington and had a long lunch with him, and when Carter expected Nyerere to ask for financial aid, all he talked about was one thing—one-man-one-vote … [Nyerere] came to Jamaica right after, gave me a long account of it. So that when Andy Young went to [Carter] about the Muzorewa thing, and pointed out the extent to which Muzorewa's agreement had deviated from the principle, in Carter's very moral mind he had already realised that this was not one-man-one-vote. And it is Nyerere who had got that into Carter's head. It's an interesting thing to remember in all that, because that was very much a factor that Mrs Thatcher must have had to take into account, and, you know, Carrington was the kind of person who would have been saying, 'The Atlantic connection, that's not going to work with you on this one, you know?'"

I shouldn't have needed Manley to say to me, as he then did, "I think it may be worth telling that story"—it was so obviously a major factor in the outcome, and I should have put it in, but I left it out as tangential. It's not tangential.

"After Carter had done that", he went on, "I would imagine that Mrs Thatcher—newly Prime Minister, very strong-minded, very strong-willed woman, would have thought, 'Well, all right, that's one of my two critical connections gone, but I still have the white Commonwealth left'." But that was wrong because Fraser *made* it wrong.

What Manley told me about the Castro connection was highly interesting too, and needs to be placed in its geopolitical setting.

"In all that, there was also the question of what, say, would radical-left Africa have to say, what might be the Cuban attitude to it, with troops in Angola, troops in Ethiopia, etcetera, etcetera, the question of whether Castro might sabotage an agreement."

The moment he said that, I could understand the concern, though it had never crossed my mind till then. Why was Soviet-aligned Cuba a military presence in Angola at that time? Obviously to support the Soviet-aligned MPLA government there against its China-aligned UNITA opponents in the field, who were backed by South Africa and the United States. To the east, in Rhodesia, Joshua Nkomo had not fought his bush war to play second fiddle to Robert Mugabe, he wanted power, or at least half of it, not a thin slice. He and his ZAPU were Moscow-aligned, Mugabe's ZANU–PF was China-aligned. Nkomo, whose core support was in the south, in Matabeleland, could safely bet that in any internationally supervised vote he would be out-polled by Mugabe's larger Shona-tribe base. Anxious about that, all he needed was some international encouragement to sabotage any deal brokered in London. Had he wanted, Nkomo could have justified a rejectionist line on a number of grounds, for instance the compromise that still ensured a white bloc in parliament, which came out of the Lancaster House conference. As it was, ZAPU launched a guerrilla war against Mugabe's government *after* independence but not before. Lacking outside assistance, the uprising was brutally crushed by the Mugabe government's Korean-trained Fifth Brigade.

I found all this intriguing at the time, more particularly because I'd never considered the Cubans in regard to Rhodesia.

"I pointed out to Malcolm," Manley told me, "that from my separate and completely… well, sort of social-democratic standpoint—notice that I had a very good relationship with Fidel, we understood each other—one of the things I could guarantee is that I could make Castro understand why the compromise, and why a settlement, and that if he wants that, fine, hands off, that would be enormously influential."

Manley told me that that was precisely what he did, "after I spoke to *her* about it, right (I remember) on the lawn in front of the place where we had the [Lusaka] weekend, and told her all about that, and you know, [Thatcher] looked at me hard, and sort of registered that point, which again had come out of a conversation between Malcolm and myself, and in fact I left from Lusaka and flew home through Havana, and spent one of these famous all-nights with Fidel where you talk all night and around six o'clock you stagger off … I took him through the whole British tradition—you know, the whole Commonwealth tradition, the way things worked, this side and the other—and because he trusted me, trusted my judgment, they never lifted a finger to upset it, and in fact supported the settlement in the end."

I should have spoken to Castro about that but it would have meant another expensive trip and I didn't have a lot of spare money in those days. It would have been important to learn, from him directly, whether the Cuban military presence in Africa at the time had potential ramifications within Rhodesia, particularly in the south; the extent to which Cuba was interested, directly or through proxies, in the rivalry between Mugabe and Nkomo and hence interested in undermining any political process likely to see Mugabe gain clear dominance; and, finally, the extent to which Castro thought Manley's drawn-out evening with him affected the equation.

While in Kingston I also interviewed Prime Minister Edward Seaga, leader of the Jamaican Labour Party. His economic policies were indisputably sounder than Manley's, though he had none of Manley's dynamism. Seaga is an important cultural figure in Jamaica, more significant in some ways than Manley. He'd played the central role in the development of an authentic Jamaican music-recording industry through the 1950s (West India Records Limited), and Higgs and Wilson, Byron Lee and the Dragonaires and others owed their wider fame to Seaga. The landslide election results from 1980 that put Seaga into power reflected very badly on Michael Manley. The only genuine populist nationalist I'd met to that point was Manley, I'd enjoyed the experience and could understand why people might follow him to Hell while guessing they'd never get back. Seaga was irrelevant to my purposes: he had nothing to do with the Mugabe ascendancy. I interviewed him out of courtesy because Fraser had written him in advance. I certainly didn't tell him I'd spent time with Manley.

The same young Rastafarian-looking taxi driver who'd driven me to my hotel several days earlier, offering to sell me a pile of *ganja* before we'd even arrived there, and then taken me to various tourist spots, also drove me back to the airport and walked with me to the check-in area where he waved to a stunningly attractive woman in her twenties, possibly Indian-Jamaican, and I waved too. He said she was flying to Germany for a couple of weeks, "all paid, some guy was here—and she don't *need* no racket boss." That much was obvious. She was on my flight but seated elsewhere, so we never got to talk.

After a stay of a couple of weeks in London, during which time I spoke with Sonny Ramphal and (on a day trip to NATO in Brussells) Carrington, I caught a British Airways plane south. First port of call was Dar es Salaam. I thought I had an appointment with Tanzania's President Julius Nyerere, then in retirement, and we'd meet somewhere in the city. I hadn't planned to stay long, just a couple of nights, and after checking into the Intercontinental Hotel I walked to his office.

"President Nyerere isn't in Dar es Salaam," the young woman behind the desk told me. "He's living in his home village in the north, up near Lake Victoria."

"Is it far?" I asked.

"Yes, far away. You would do best to fly to Mwanza, then hire a Land-Rover, and someone from the village could perhaps meet you half-way."

"Couldn't I just rent a car here and drive up there?"

She discouraged that enterprise.

"Are there regular flights to Mwanza?"

She nodded, "But I don't know how often."

Given that I had a flight securely booked out of Dar es Salaam for Harare, and appointments set up in Harare and Lusaka for the following week; that, even if I took a plane to Mwanza, I knew nothing of the condition of the roads up around Lake Victoria; and that I had no idea how one hires a Land-Rover in Mwanza, I decided to give Julius Nyerere a miss. Yes, he was an important player in the Zimbabwe set-up, and I'd long been interested in his African socialism with its concomitant economic consequences, its achievements in literacy and health care, and its relation to the traditional culture. His devout Catholicism, daily attendance at Mass and regular fasting added to my interest, but the sum total came up short. I told the lady I was grateful for her help.

Sitting in the Air Tanzania Boeing 737 waiting to take off from the airport, I struck up a conversation with the fellow seated next to me. He asked where I was going and I said that after Harare and Lusaka I'd be flying to Johannesburg.

"You have *two* passports?" he asked.

"No, actually I have *one* passport."

"Can I see it?"

The request seemed odd but I complied, withdrawing it from my inside jacket pocket and passing it to him. He turned its pages.

"You have a South African *visa*!"

"Well, yes … I'll need it. Got it in London."

He looked across to the left and back, to the other side of the plane.

"That elderly lady there, see her? Two rows back? Well, they wouldn't let her into Tanzania. She's just spent a week at the airport, sleeping on a bench. I was speaking with her earlier. She's like you, she's only *got* one passport, with a South African visa in it. That's why they wouldn't let her in. You're very lucky, or someone's watching over you."

Then, explaining that Mugabe needed all the economic connections with South Africa he could get, he assured me there'd be no issues over visas at Harare's airport.

The next appointment was with President Kenneth Kaunda of Zambia, but I'd decided to base myself in Harare, make a one-day return flight to Lusaka to interview Kaunda, and then immediately return to Harare to interview Mugabe.

I took an up-scale room at Meikles Hotel with park views and followed the usual routine—unpacked, ironed some stuff, took a shower, pulled on a fresh pair of cream linen slacks, blue-striped button-down shirt, navy blazer, poured myself some whisky from the minibar, topped it with soda and ice, and sampled it. Then I walked across to the telephone and dialled an Australian couple living near the University of Zimbabwe, not far from the home of Robert Mugabe.

I didn't know them, but I'd met their daughter in Melbourne at my friend Ian Crawford's place. The husband, originally from Perth, had been sent from Australia to Rhodesia during the Second World War for advanced aircrew training under the Empire Air Training Scheme prior to joining the RAF in Britain, and had returned to Rhodesia after the war to take up tobacco farming near the Mozambique border. Having sold the plantation, he and his wife had retired to Harare. They'd have liked to return to Perth, but were unable to get their capital out of Zimbabwe, a common story in southern Africa, including South Africa at the time. Conditions in Harare struck me as good, and my new friends, at whose home I dined that night, were only moderately critical of the government.

The one-hour flight to Lusaka passed to the north of the Kariba Dam—I could see it out to the left from 30,000 feet. I was wearing a navy suit and travelling light, a pigskin bag supplemented by the usual effects: Sony Walkman Professional tape recorder, headphones for playback, notebook and pen, passport, address book, wallet with American dollars in three denominations, credit cards, calling cards, driver's licence, Leica IIIF, polarised sunglasses, couple of cigars and a matchbook. Following arrival formalities I took a taxi to State House, paid the fare plus a tip that doubled it, walked inside and glanced around. Almost immediately, an official approached, introduced herself and led me to an office adjacent to the President's, where I sat down and waited.

Like Tanzania, Zambia at the time was a one-party state, deeply in debt, with copper prices on the slide and discontent brewing in the streets. Later, under popular pressure, the country would transition to multi-party democracy. However, following independence from colonial rulers, who had governed in the interests of their capital investments and never democratically, most African states initially or fairly quickly adopted one-party systems and socialist economies, and most joined the Non-Aligned Movement, wishing to keep both sides of the Cold War at a political remove while welcoming economic relations and controlled investment. They'd inherited borders drawn up by Western nations without much respect for tribal and religious divisions, so these countries were easy prey for big powers with their divide-and-control instincts. Two common arguments for the one-party state at that early stage of post-colonial development were national unity and the prevention of outside manipulation of internal divisions, whether by Washington, London, Paris or Moscow, of the kind exemplified disastrously in the Congo in the early 1960s.

Kaunda, son of a Presbyterian minister, had, like his father, been a schoolteacher before becoming active in the Northern Rhodesian African National Congress through the early 1950s. Later, in 1958, he formed the more radical Zambian African National Congress, banned the following year. After spending time in prison, in early 1960 he assumed leadership of the newly-formed United National Independence

Party and, through reformed electoral processes recently set up under the government of Sir Roy Welensky, became Prime Minster prior to independence. With independence secured on 24 October 1964, Kaunda became President and remained so until 1991 when he gave in to internal and external pressures for multi-party elections that saw his defeat. After losing power he spent some time under house arrest. As President he oversaw the rapid development of educational institutions (minimal prior to independence), infrastructure and manufacturing, and established Zambian control over mining and other foreign interests. Through the 1970s his rule became increasingly autocratic. It was based on what he termed Zambian Humanism, which blended socialism, religion and local traditions of social morality.

He was a significant figure in the Non-Aligned Movement, the recognised leader of the Front-Line States bordering South Africa, and supported neighbouring guerrilla organisations fighting for majority rule in Rhodesia, Angola, Mozambique, South Africa and South-West Africa, some of which were allowed to maintain encampments inside Zambia's borders. Deeply religious, he nevertheless recognised (in his 1980 book *The Riddle of Violence*) that "With some exceptions, the power which establishes a state is violence; the power which maintains it is violence; the power which eventually overthrows it is violence." He had in mind the necessity of a police force and a military, and one recalls Hobbes's observation on the ultimate sanction of state violence (the hangman at the end of the corridor), without which there's no order. It's not easy to think of a state for which Kaunda's claim is false. The Soviet Union is an exception on the third count. The United States, Australia, and every other settler state on earth qualify on the first two counts. Kaunda himself had used military force to prevent the slaughter of one tribe by another.

After a short wait I was ushered in. He was 61 at the time, wearing a short-sleeved, off-white, linen Kariba suit with shirt but without tie, a couple of pens in the left breast pocket, copper bracelet on his left wrist, no wristwatch. We shook hands and he motioned me to a seat beside his desk, on top of which I placed the tape recorder. He also had one, out of sight, because in addition to a pile of books and a Satinex tissue-dispenser there were two microphones on the desk, one pointing at him and the other towards me, their leads running down and off somewhere beyond the woven carpet that underlay his desk. Behind Kaunda and to my left was a bookcase containing reference works including *Africa Who's Who*, *Africa Today*, *Makers of Modern Africa*, *Contemporary Leaders of Africa*, *Roget's Thesaurus*, *Brewer's Dictionary of Phrase & Fable*, a couple of sets of encyclopedias including the Treccani *Enciclopedia del Novecento*, and 40-odd volumes of *Lenin: Collected Works* bending their shelves. The Treccani and the Lenin were probably gifts from the Italians and Soviets. On the uppermost shelf were figurines, a bronze bust of JFK, a book on Non-Alignment with a cover shot of Nasser, Nehru and Tito together. Against the wall behind me and to the left was a Japanese ceremonial sword with a tassel hanging from its hilt—another gift. As we were on the point of beginning our conversation an official took a photograph, sharp even through a Nikon 7X watchmaker's lens.

I pressed *Record* and asked the first question, a long one, and at first he didn't answer. Instead he put an observation and a question of his own.

"You have such a wonderful composure. May I call you Philip?"

Never paid that compliment before, I acceded. How could I dislike such a man? He won me in six words. One word.

We talked about his role during and prior to the 1979 Commonwealth Heads of Government Meeting in Lusaka, and in the Mugabe ascendancy, all of which I later put into print. He had a lot of respect for Margaret

Thatcher, personally liked her, and thought Fraser's role "very key," explaining why. But the most telling part of the interview came when I asked him to estimate the chances of the Commonwealth-appointed Eminent Persons Group, then in South Africa, successfully initiating a political process between the Nationalist Party Government and the African National Congress and other outlawed opposition groups. He was pessimistic.

"I've been dealing with South Africans for the last 61 years—because they were *here*, Philip, they controlled Northern Rhodesia then. There were only mines, and Afrikaans controlled our country's industry here, about two thousand of them. So really, we know something about them. And they left, almost in a bloc when the time of independence was getting near."

Watching him, I could see he was talking about something personal. He knew these people and the memories were bad.

"They told you where you belonged. 'You are an Englishman? Well then, we know who *you* are, and we can discuss this over a cup of tea.' If you were an African it was 'I *hate* you—get out of here, you're a *Kaffir*.' That's what we had to experience here. So we know something about them. But there's something else …"

He then reminded me how the Voortrekkers, when threatened by hostile tribes, would draw the wagons around themselves in a circular *laager*, firing out from inside, practically invulnerable.

"They have *developed* that *laager* mentality," he told me. "They've locked themselves up, and unfortunately it's a deliberate and rather conscious decision to do that, because they see that as the way to salvation. So it will take a lot to change them from where they are, and we don't have the time.

"But God's power works many ways. It could be that his kindness works towards solving the situation *that* way. Now, normally, I wouldn't expect much, but I'm praying for a miracle myself, if only for fear of what will happen if this [Commonwealth-initiated process] doesn't succeed."

After I switched off the tape recorder he told me "God is very close to us." I'd been away from home for over a month and for reasons I won't go into I took note of what he said. He'd recognised something that wasn't composed and this was his way of saying he'd seen it. It was obviously intended as a take-away and I carried it with me on the flight back to Harare. Evangelicals call it the Word of Knowledge. It's rare, and I certainly don't have it.

Robert Mugabe was brought up and educated as a Catholic and the influence was deep. When Kaunda speaks of God to someone like me or more publicly, he talks as one would expect of a Protestant, of a God known directly and intimately, unmediated by any institution, whereas Mugabe has little to say publicly about God in that way but admires Catholicism's institutional forms, its top–down authority structure and the Jesuit order by which he was educated. He's paid his respects to the Pope more than once. In addition to their Christianity Kaunda and Mugabe share a belief in socialism with African characteristics, but Kaunda's socialism is less doctrinaire, Mugabe's ostensibly Marxist–Leninist—ostensibly, because he has never attempted to communise Zimbabwe. There has of course been the dispossession of most of the white farmers, often by violent means, the transfer of those lands to ZANU-PF cadres and other black Zimbabweans, and the severe economic consequences of that, exacerbated by London- and Washington-enforced economic sanctions. Mugabe gave the process the go-ahead after twenty years of resisting the move, buckling to intense pressure from his base, fighters who were promised land during the bush war and then for twenty years never given it. He delivered to save his neck. His suppression of Nkomo's forces in the south was ruthless and accompanied by atrocities committed by the notorious Fifth Brigade. To what extent their methodology was ordered by Mugabe can't be known, but he bears responsibility. There was a Swiss bank account in the relatively modest sum of seven figures connected to him through his first wife—not exactly a planeload of gold.

His first degree, in 1951, was a Bachelor of Arts from Fort Hare in South Africa, after which he studied for and was awarded another six degrees through distance education, including during a decade's imprisonment in Rhodesia between 1964 and 1974: Bachelor of Administration, Bachelor of Education (both from the University of South Africa), Bachelor of Science, Bachelor of Laws, Master of Laws (all from the University of London), and finally, also from the University of London, his seventh degree, Master of Science, during his premiership of Zimbabwe.

I spoke with him, six years into his power, in the old ZANU-PF headquarters in Harare, in an ordinary room sparsely furnished, at a table devoid of ornaments. I was shown in, Mugabe entered from another door and welcomed me and we sat down. As far as I know he didn't record the interview, but my own recording is as sharp as it was in 1986. He was dressed in a navy blue suit, white shirt and maroon tie, showed courtesy, answered questions frankly, with intellectual respect, thoughtfully and at length, drawing subtle distinctions, putting qualifications. Because he was not a participant at the 1979 Lusaka heads-of-government meeting that created the process that led to the elections that brought him to power, he couldn't speak much about its background except from what he'd learned later. Nevertheless, what he told me about his attitudes at the time, the pressures on him from the Front-Line States to fall in with the Lusaka agreement, and follow-up pressures on him at a subsequent Non-Aligned meeting in Havana, was very frank. I knew nothing about the significance of the Havana meeting.

Mugabe's feeling, the feeling of ZANU–PF, in the lead-up to Lusaka was that in her support for the Muzorewa–Smith government Margaret Thatcher was not only going to end up on the losing side, "nor did we feel that she was on the legal side. The legal side was our side. We were fighting to dislodge Ian Smith, to undo UDI [Smith's Unilateral Declaration of Independence of 11 November 1965], however much she might have disagreed with us on the form of the struggle we were waging. But nevertheless we felt that we were fighting an illegal government in order to bring about legality."

As part of that attitude "We had refused that negotiations should ever take place between us and the Ian Smith regime," and for that reason, Mugabe told me, he and his party "were not very happy at the stance that was being adopted" at Lusaka by Kaunda, Nyerere, Manley, Fraser and others on that side.

"Our own view, which was the view of nationalists of course, revolutionaries, which tends to be quite decided in its extreme viewpoint, was not in every case the view of even the Front-Line States [principally Angola, Mozambique, Tanzania and Zambia]. The Front-Line States, I suppose, wanted a kind of compromise situation where the British Government would convene a conference, chair that conference and lead the country to the democratic process of an election."

The idea of coming to power via a conference and elections was counter to ZANU–PF's and PF–ZAPU's *raison d'être*, even if they thought it would succeed, which they didn't. "We were bent on prosecuting the struggle, we were doing very well, and we didn't see any reason why a political solution should be sought when a military solution was yielding the results that we were getting." Nevertheless they agreed to go to a conference between all the parties at Lancaster House in London.

Yet Mugabe and Joshua Nkomo continued a line of maximum resistance on what they considered key principles, particularly the future of the Rhodesian Army and their opposition to the inclusion of the Muzorewa–Smith government in the negotiations. This resistance could certainly have derailed the London conference, due to begin on 10 September 1979, in its earliest stages. In fact the resistance continued for fully another month after the Lusaka conference, right into the Sixth Conference of the Non-Aligned Movement in Havana from 3 to 9 September 1979. It was there that the leaders of two Front-Line States bordering Zimbabwe, Kenneth Kaunda and Samora Machel of Mozambique, together with Julius Nyerere, in a private meeting with Mugabe and Nkomo (who were there representing the "Patriotic Front of Zimbabwe"), won the necessary further compromises. This meant that Lancaster House would be a more straightforward process; it also meant, incidentally, that the Havana Conference lent its support to the Lancaster House process without qualification.[6]

"We wondered at the change," Mugabe told me. "They did not want us any more to insist that the Rhodesian forces must not be part of the national army, when the moment came for us to re-establish the army. And they were for this comprehensive meeting, which would include the Rhodesian side. But after asking questions we said, 'Well, fine, we have no choice, let's play that down.'" These were last-minute concessions—the Lancaster House conference was scheduled to begin the day after

6 *6th Summit Conference of Heads of State or Government of the Non-Aligned Movement, Havana, Cuba, 3–9 September 1979*, Political Declaration, paragraphs 51–60. http://cns.miis.edu/nam/documents/Official_Document/6th_Summit_FD_Havana_Declaration_1979_Whole.pdf. Sourced 13 April 2019.

the Havana meeting ended, so that in order to be there Mugabe and Nkomo had to leave Havana early.

"So there it was, we had to make compromises at Lancaster House. Really, it was a big compromise for us to agree to a political solution where we had wanted things to be determined militarily at the end, we were [determined] not to have anything to do with those who had caused UDI or who had supported it, directly or indirectly, and we were [determined] not to compromise on the land issue at all, but Lancaster House brought about those compromises, and in the final analysis it brought us independence."

Mugabe told me he thought it important that Fraser had declared his opposition to United States interference in Angola, specifically its covert aid to the UNITA forces of Jonas Savimbi. "It's a serious matter," he explained. "For the whole of Africa it poses a real threat. You see, what it means is that if the United States does not accept your government or its ideology then it can assist the opposition outrightly. That's the writing on the wall for all of us, and it's a really big blunder that the United States is committing."

I switched off the tape recorder. It hadn't been an unpleasant experience. Maybe there was a cup of tea thrown in, I can't recall. I *can* say that there's nothing unreasonable or crazy on that tape, and of course Zimbabwe was still in good shape in 1986. There was no strong reason at that time to question the processes and personalities that facilitated his ascent to power, which would inevitably have been his in any case. I thanked him, he escorted me out and wished me well. He struck me as self-contained, admirably composed, and I wondered whether Kaunda had ever told him that.

4

On the Road with Antonin Scalia

I spent a couple of days with United States Supreme Court Justice Antonin Scalia in 2011, but I'd first met him five years earlier. In October 2005 a two-day seminar had been held in Melbourne, organised by Claudio Véliz on behalf of the Boston, Melbourne, Oxford *Conversazioni* on Culture and Society around the topic of "Judicial Activism: Power without Responsibility?" Eminent jurists and constitutional lawyers spoke, including two of the seven justices of the High Court of Australia (Michael Kirby and Dyson Heydon) and, more remarkably, two of the nine justices on the United States Supreme Court: Stephen Breyer (a Clinton appointee) and Scalia (a Reagan appointee).

Never, as far as I'm aware, had there been an assembly of jurists in this country that included close to a quarter of the United States Supreme Court, and it's a testimony to Claudio Véliz's pulling power among his international friends that he—he alone—was able to bring them half way around the world for the occasion. Scalia was the most conservative judge on the U. S. Supreme Court, an originalist (his term) in his interpretation of the United States Constitution, always trying to read it as written and understood by its framers, whereas Breyer, on the liberal side politically, was more sympathetic to creative interpretations of a text conceived by progressives as "open" rather than closed or "dead"—as Scalia liked to put it, "I defend a *dead* Constitution". Naturally they took opposing sides in the debate on whether unelected judges should get involved in changing the law as opposed to leaving that work to the democratically elected members of Congress.

Courtesy of Claudio I'd met Justice Breyer even earlier, in Boston in 2001 during my time at Boston University as Visiting Professor within the University Professors' Program, a section created by University President John Silber and headed for twelve years by Claudio, who had no fewer than four Nobel Prize-winners under his purview. Stephen Breyer is quiet and consensus-seeking. I'd shared a light dinner with him as part of a small group prior to a concert we attended at Boston's Symphony Hall. Tables were by invitation and our group had one of them. Most would find it easy to get along with Breyer.

On the other hand Scalia, though witty and congenial, tended to divide people. When I first met him in 2005 he at once struck me as the more interesting of the two, partly because his ideas were so forthright, sharply defined and challenging, but also because the paper he presented to us in 2005 was immensely entertaining in its merciless demolition of judicial activism. For many of us it was the highlight of the *Conversazione*. To understand why five years later I would enjoy his company, consider the paper he presented in 2005.

Its title was provocative in the extreme, expressly designed to trigger his opponents: "Mullahs of the West: Judges as Authoritative

Expositors of the Natural Law". Unkind? Indeed. Untrue? Well now, the Mullahs of Iran are certainly the expositors of Islamic law, which in an unorthodox way, according to many scholars, acknowledges a natural law. But judges on a constitutional court—how are they, in Scalia's view, "expositors of the natural law"? In fact the title has some validity, as his paper went on to show. In the march of progress through America's twentieth century there grew a belief in the authority of the expert. From a hundred unelected federal commissions and boards these experts, as distinct from the electorate and their deputies in Congress, determined what was right. Beyond mid-century the experts gradually fell into disrepute because the issues they were "settling" were *not* settled but still widely debated, like most complex issues, and the debate would not be shut down. But while the experts were losing the electorate's trust, Scalia argued, a new wielder of power was in the ascendancy:

> the judge-moralist. Whereas *technical* questions, we have come to learn, do not have any single right answer, surely *moral* questions do. Whether a woman has a natural right to an abortion. Whether society has a right to take a man's life for his crimes. Whether it is unfair (and hence, in the terminology of the American Constitution, a denial of "equal protection") to permit marriage between people of opposite sexes, but not between people of the same sex. Whether a human being has an unalienable right to take his own life, and to have the assistance of others in doing so. These, and many similar questions, involve basic morality, basic human rights—and *surely* there is a right and wrong answer to them.
>
> Well, I believe firmly that indeed there is. That is to say, I believe in natural law. The problem is that my view of what the natural law prescribes is quite different from others' views—and none of us has any means of demonstrating, with anything approaching scientific certainty, the correctness of his position. Thus, as a matter of democratic theory, there is no more reason to take *these* issues away from the people than there is to take away issues of economic policy.

In other words Scalia was saying that the legislature, reflecting the popular will, is the appropriate authority to decide such issues, not unelected judges, who have no more right to decide them than Joe Six-Pack, whose representatives in Congress actually *do* have that right delegated to them democratically. So yes, "Mullahs of the West". And the range of their moral purview is practically unlimited. On the Supreme Court, Scalia told his audience, "We have held it impermissible for a state to maintain a military college for men only, despite the fact that West Point, the Citadel and the Virginia Military Institute had for more than a century not been thought to be in violation of the Constitution's requirement of equal protection of the law."

Things change, and so, some think, does the United States Constitution. Its meaning is assumed by prominent liberal judges and academic lawyers to be *flexible*, almost infinitely so. Over the past half-dozen decades the Court has developed the concept of a "living Constitution" whose meaning can change over time to suit "the evolving standards of decency that mark the progress of a maturing society"[7], a hopeful view of human nature that assumes that the twentieth century was morally superior to the nineteenth, or the Soviet system to the Czarist, or the Third Reich to the Second. In passing, Scalia took a swing at one of the other paper-givers, the Australian academic constitutional lawyer Professor Michael Coper. "I do not think it is an open question, as Professor Coper does, whether the courts or the legislature should be the preferred agent of change—not, at least, if change is to be in the direction desired *by the people*. Anyone who thinks that the country's most prominent lawyers reflect the views of the people needs a reality check." Professor Coper, Scalia thought, had an inflated idea of the "power of criticism" to keep judges in line—and *whose* criticism would that be?

7 *Trop v. Dulles*, 356 U.S. 86 (1958).

That of a secondary contingent, equally unrepresentative, intellectually superior in their own conceit, living off the judgment-makers by writing about and about them. "I do not *want* my judges to heed criticism. They are given life tenure precisely to enable them to do their duty in the teeth of criticism. What I do want, however, is the selection of judges who view it as their role to abide by the texts that the people have adopted, and in the sense that the people intended."[8] The intellectual force and wit that Scalia brought to bear on the subject of debate energised the audience, whether they were *prima facie* sympathetic or not, and received sustained applause. It was a paper he would give over and over in the months that followed, in the United States and Europe,[9] and its first major outing was at this *Conversazione*.

Five-and-a-bit years later, in February 2011, Scalia was in Australia again, and on this occasion I was asked to collect him from his hotel and drive him to the Vélizes' spectacularly-sited house below Cinema Point, on the Great Ocean Road a few kilometres before Lorne, spend the night there, and next day show him around the most scenic stretches of Victoria's south-west coast. Over a couple of days I got to know him passably well. I was given very short notice, but I managed to read up on him in a rudimentary way in order to be conversable. I didn't read any of his opinions, but I read *about* some of them. I also read about his background.

Born on 11 March 1936 in Trenton, New Jersey, he was the only child of Salvatore Eugene and Catherine Louise Scalia. Salvatore Scalia had immigrated to the United States from Sommatino in Sicily as a

8 Antonin Scalia, "Mullahs of the West: Judges as Authoritative Expositors of the Natural Law?", The Sir John Young Oration, in *Judicial Activism: Power without Responsibility?*, The Boston, Melbourne, Oxford Conversazioni on Culture and Society, ed. Benjamin Kiely, Trinity College, University of Melbourne (Melbourne, 2006), pp. 63–70.

9 See Bruce Allen Murphy, *Scalia: A Court of One* (Simon & Schuster, New York, 2014), Chapter 19, "The Dead Constitution Tour", pp. 336–353.

boy and later taught romance languages at Brooklyn College. Antonin's mother, of Italian parentage, taught elementary school. Antonin, or Nino, attended public and Jesuit schools, undertook a degree in history at Georgetown University and went on to study law at Harvard, with outstanding results at each stage of the ascent. I knew all this by the time I was on my way to pick him up, and knew too that he was a conservative with populist leanings.

Accordingly at the appointed hour I drove into the circular concourse of the Sofitel Hotel near the top of Melbourne's Collins Street and pulled up by the hotel's ingress, where I could see Scalia, with that squarish head, neutral expression of his, and solid, overburdened frame, of medium height, in casual attire, sitting there waiting for me. I climbed out and walked over and we did our introductions. He asked me to call him Nino. I unlocked the car's boot, pushed his suitcase in, pressed the lid shut and opened the passenger door for him. I was using a base-model, good-order, five-year-old Toyota because my newer Honda was being serviced and my Alfa roadster was too small to accommodate anyone as stocky as Scalia and his effects.

His first comment inside the car, even before we were rolling, was "Crank windows! I haven't seen crank windows in forty years!" I apologised: "You'll just have to *wind* it up and down." I was thinking "He's not paying for this trip, which wasn't my idea, he just sort of came my way, and immediately he's criticising the car". But I also thought he had a point, that the car *wasn't* suitable, that he had serious rank, that when the President's delivering the State of the Union Address this chap's sitting with his judicial colleagues right up at the front. I should have *rented* something better, damn it, and certainly something with electric windows—and electrically reclining seats, as it turned out.

We drove out across the two-and-a-half-kilometres-long West

Gate Bridge and I told him about the 1970 disaster there: how, during construction, there was a major structural failure and an entire box-girder span, a couple of thousand tons, dropped 160 feet in a flat splat onto the muddy ground below, killing the thirty-five men who were either on it or lunching in huts beneath. "You can imagine the result". He said he was already trying to forget it.

With the bridge in the rear view mirror, the road levelled out and we were on the way to Geelong and beyond. Until he dozed off we talked about his previous trips to Australia, which seemed to have been mostly or entirely vacation. He said he loved the place but didn't go into much detail, or any detail I can now recall. After the trip I made some notes, mainly of things he'd said, knowing I might write this up at some stage. He questioned me about Claudio and Maria-Isabel so I told him about their backgrounds, about Boston University and joining Stephen Breyer at Symphony Hall. I can't recall anything else about that first leg of the trip except his sleeping through half of it. The road to Geelong is boring, as I'd warned him in advance, provoking the question "Have you been to Nebraska?"

That night we dined with Claudio and Maria-Isabel to the accompaniment of breakers crashing across the rock ledges hundreds of feet below. Over dinner Scalia introduced the subject of Chile, particularly the Pinochet regime. By way of background, Maria Isabel told him about growing up on her father's extensive *viña* in the Central Valley and in the old family house there, and how one day in 1971 or 1972 the entire property was occupied without warning by agricultural workers armed with sickles—it was what they called a *toma* or takeover. She talked about the social chaos under Salvador Allende's democratically elected socialist government, whose extreme-left allies were beyond Allende's control, the lawless *tomas* up and down the country, the consequent reaction by armed elements on the radical right including *Patria y Libertad*, the daily demonstrations, counter-demonstrations and tear gas, the spiralling of violence and—last straw for the Vélizes—the occupation by radical students of Claudio's prestigious Institute of International Studies, which he'd created within the University of Chile. But it was clear that Scalia already knew about the preconditions of the 1973 military *coup*, and he expressed no criticism of it. In the early 1970s, as I knew from the little I'd read about him, he'd been a junior member of the Nixon administration, so it didn't surprise me that he knew about Chile or that his sympathies were where they were, not that he'd had anything to do with foreign affairs—among other things he'd been Assistant Attorney-General for Nixon's Office of Legal Counsel, in which position he'd continued under Gerald Ford.

The house at Cinema Point has a guest wing with two bedrooms, a bathroom and independent facilities for making breakfast. Scalia and I slept across there, but in the morning as soon as we'd showered we went back into the central section for breakfast, where he showed us something none of us knew till then: how to boil eggs so that they're always soft inside. Asked what he wanted, he said he liked a couple of soft-boiled eggs for breakfast, so Maria-Isabel placed two eggs in a saucepan and half-filled it with cold water. "No, not that way!" he told her. "If you want to have soft-boiled eggs *don't start them in cold water*! Here—let me take the eggs out." So he removed the saucepan from the cook-top, fished the eggs from the still-cold water and replaced the saucepan on the stove, then waited till it came to a vigorous boil. "Now we lower it to a simmer, see?—and only *now* do we place the eggs into the water, thus, and thus. I like to leave them in there for four minutes, or a bit longer if you're doing three or four eggs at a time. You *always* have soft-centred eggs this way." So never again did any of us three do boiled eggs any other way. It's not a trivial matter, eggs are too expensive to mistreat, and I owe him for the information.

Over breakfast, which we had out on the deck, by way of asking him about his Sicilian background Maria Isabel told him she was a devoted Catholic, and from then on the conversation was about the evils of Vatican II, the liberal theologians hard at work disintegrating Catholic beliefs, the beauties of the Tridentine rite and the old Latin liturgy, and the importance of finding a good church with truly-believing priests and attending Mass *there*.

“The modernists love to tell you that you should attend Mass at your local parish church”, he said. “They don’t want you shopping around and voting with your feet, that’s what *that’s* about, and these days there’s a good chance your local parish priest is deep into heresy.” Nothing I heard him say over two days was bland, and if there was nothing worth saying he shut up.

“I’m informed”, I told him, “that there’s a Catholic church in Brisbane where witches congregate mid-week. A parishioner told me.”

“I’d believe it.”

“Claudio’s a Calvinist” Maria-Isabel told him.

“They have a clear and logical theology”, Scalia said, “or they used to.”

I told him I was born into Lutheranism, read myself half-way into Catholicism and was reading my way out *via* the newspapers. He didn’t like that at all and said the institution was what mattered, not individuals—the usual answer. I couldn’t be bothered, it was a sunny morning on the deck, dozens of cockatoos were circling and screeching or fighting each other off the feeding trays, while half a dozen kookaburras stood on the railings waiting to be hand-fed chunks of rump steak.

After a couple of coffees I saw Scalia into the car and we drove up the steep gravel drive, onto the bitumen road and down around the sweeping curves of Big Hill to Lorne—however, instead of going through town and along the coast I turned right and drove across the Otway Ranges. My idea, I explained, was to do the ocean-side drive from the other end, travelling by inland roads to Port Campbell and then returning by the Great Ocean Road from there, so that we wouldn't be travelling out and back by the same route. That was a mistake.

After descending the ranges at Deans Marsh we took a back road that runs down along creek valleys and then up and across undulating country before getting into the back streets of the light-industrial city of Colac, which can't easily be avoided. After that we were back on a main highway and suddenly into the Stony Rises, an inhospitable, rocky and convoluted volcanic landscape some people find interesting (the mid-nineteenth-century landscapist Eugene von Guerard did a picture there), emerging fifteen minutes later into the rich pastoral flatlands around Camperdown where dormant volcanic mountains give visual relief to the monotony of the plains.

We talked about the law. I knew he was fairly literalist in his constitutional readings, but he didn't *call* it literalism, he told me, he called it originalism or textualism. He said the United States Constitution was a document whose meanings were *ipso facto* those originally intended by its framers, and it should be so read and applied. One should read the Constitution *as written*. If it was silent on some issue, it shouldn't be tortured to speak on it. Knowing that his father had been a literary critic attached to the New Criticism school of close textual analysis, and being aware of what those critics called the intentional fallacy, I asked Scalia how he went about ascertaining the intentions of the framers of the Constitution, a collaborative work by men of varying beliefs and attitudes. He appreciated the question because it gave him the chance to elaborate on his method. I can't recall all the details he went into but I remember some of them. He said that for any particular Constitutional section or amendment affecting a specific case he was sitting on, he would study the informing contexts of the time, the earliest edition of Webster's Dictionary, the correspondence of the framers wherever relevant to the particular text—that sort of thing. And, he added, it was generally patently obvious what *wasn't* intended.

We discovered a common interest in rifles and shooting, a sport both of us had enjoyed since boyhood. It arose from a topic I introduced in relation to one of the two cases I'd made a point of reading about prior to meeting him, a Second Amendment case, *District of Columbia v. Heller.*[10] The other was the landmark abortion case, *Roe v. Wade*[11] *(about which he said little, except that it should be overturned and handed back to the States).* I particularly wanted to hear him talk about the Second Amendment to the American Constitution, which reads: *"A well regulated Militia, being necessary to the security of a free State, the right of the people to keep and bear Arms, shall not be infringed".*

For some people it's primarily about *"a well regulated Militia"*, not a generalised right *"to keep and bear Arms"*, but in Heller the majority of the Court, concurring with Scalia, interpreted the right in its widest sense. I told him I hadn't read his opinion in the case, and he told me I should do so as it was a good example of his originalism in practice. Subsequently I've put that right. In its deconstruction of the two grammatical parts of the Amendment—the prefatory part and the operative part—it's a model of the close textual analysis his father as a New Critic would have appreciated, reinforced by the contemporary contextual evidence Scalia brought to bear. He read the text as affirming and protecting a *pre-existing*

10 *District of Columbia v. Heller*, 554 U.S. 570 (2008).

11 *Roe v. Wade*, 410 U.S. 113 (1973).

right to *individual self-defence*, not about membership of a State militia. The ruling's affirmation of *an individual right to self-defence*, he told me, was one of his proudest achievements on the Court. That the right was *pre-existing* was of course adequately manifested in the words "will not be infringed". Something can only be infringed if it already exists. He added "Can you imagine anyone in Appalachia in the late eighteenth century, say Daniel Boone, having his right to his rifle denied? It's nuts."

He asked me what I shot. I said I didn't hunt game, though my best rifle was a Scottish deer rifle, a Daniel Fraser Mannlicher in .256 calibre, and that I had friends and relations who hunted. I'd done some trap shooting including skeet. I told him that at seventeen I belonged to a long-established rifle club and shot on the Dean Range at Port Adelaide over distances up to 800 yards. I'd carry my .303 Lee Enfield No. 4 Mk 1 rifle with me out to the Port and back on the train, not even in a bag or case, just holding it propped between my legs. None of the other passengers saw anything odd in it. He liked that and told me that he himself had belonged to a small-bore rifle club as a boy, in New York City, and that he too had openly carried his rifle to the matches on public transport.

I couldn't believe we were having this conversation. If anybody had told me twenty years ago that one day I'd be talking like this to a Justice of the United States Supreme Court I'd have said they were crazy.

He said he hunted fowl and four-legged game. I asked whether he hunted deer and he replied "I like to hunt black bear." I asked him "Where?" and he said black bear was found all through the eastern states and much of the country besides. You could hunt them in the autumn and the spring. He told me there were almost certainly more black bears in North America now than when Europeans first settled. The creatures raided farms where sources of food were at hand, they sometimes tore people to pieces but mostly they weren't out to be aggressive. You could hunt them through the woods, you could hunt them from hides, you could bait them. If you hunted them on foot you had to keep upwind as their sense of smell was acute. I remember thinking to myself "You don't look in a condition to be hunting them at all, and certainly not through the woods on foot". I asked what calibre he used on them and he replied "Thirty-ought-six". This was the 30-06 cartridge, used by the U.S. military through much of the twentieth century, a medium calibre for centre-fire rifles. I had no direct experience of it myself but I knew it was good for a range of game from white-tail deer through to buffalo, and I commented "That's a good all-round calibre". He replied "Yes, but not for quail". I remember precisely where he said it, between Cobden and Port Campbell along a stretch of the Curdies River valley lined with Lombardy poplars.

At Port Campbell we parked the car and I took him into The Waves, the only proper restaurant in the town, with an attractive little bar and a decent menu. I'm dredging up memories of the place as I write but I'm not inventing. He certainly paid, because I clearly remember him preventing me from paying. I had fish as I always do in there; I have no memory of what he ordered, but I distinctly recall ordering a bottle of Riesling while he was away from the table and otherwise engaged. I almost certainly would have started with a whisky and soda even though I had responsibilities with such a passenger. I have no recollection whatsoever of what we talked about in there. The table at which we sat was the one located beside the window on the southern side of the restaurant, if anyone cares. Somewhere or other, but not in there I think, we talked about the death penalty, which he said was certainly not "cruel and unusual" when the Constitution was written, though he couldn't say he was particularly in favour of it. That was properly a matter for legislatures, not a constitutional court. One of us said (I think it was him) that if life had the supreme value there'd be no higher value for which to sacrifice one's life. Anyway there was agreement on that.

We left the restaurant and drove west to Peterborough where he photographed the Bay of Islands, then a U-turn and back east through Port Campbell to the Loch Ard Gorge, scene of a disastrous shipwreck in 1878, where he walked all about the place photographing the scene from three sides and from the sands below. Then it was on to the Twelve Apostles, sandstone monoliths a few hundred metres out from shore. We pulled into the extensive car park on the landward side of the road and walked across to the viewing areas where he took more photographs. On the way back to the car we called in at the men's lavatories and stood side-by-side for about a minute. I walked out and waited. It was a long time till he emerged, full of compliments.

From the Twelve Apostles to Apollo Bay it's a long stretch of mainly mountainous road, with little apart from forest to see, and he certainly didn't see it. Lunch had done for him. He figured out the way to manually lower the back of his seat and within a minute he was sound asleep. An hour and more later, between Apollo Bay and Lorne, where the road is at its most beautiful, he was sleeping still. Entirely refreshed by the time we got to Lorne, he went into the newsagency there and bought a collection of booklets on the region and when we came out I asked someone to photograph us beside the car. It was late afternoon when we got back to South Main, in time for cocktails, a South American dinner on the deck in the dusk, and then an early night's sleep across in the guest wing.

Because I frequently glanced at him over at least an hour and a half between the Twelve Apostles and Lorne, semi-reclined in a profound sleep, I can imagine what he looked like five years later when he was found dead, flat on his back with his head propped up by pillows. He died in his sleep during the night of 12–13 February 2016 at a 30,000-

acre hunting resort, the Cibolo Creek Ranch in West Texas (location for the 1956 film *Giant*). He'd gone to bed early following an afternoon's quail shoot and didn't appear for his breakfast of boiled eggs. There was no sign of struggle or disarray. He died of natural causes, not of a heart attack but of some cause or complex of causes unknown (he had many health issues). There was no autopsy, which fuelled conspiracy theories. If there was a conspiracy it didn't work, because President Trump has replaced him with another originalist, Neil Gorsuch. It was general comment at the time that for Scalia it was the best exit, given his passion for hunting. I thought so when I heard the news. It's gratifying to have photographs of a couple of days together, with him looking on top of things, more or less.

Claudio Véliz at Harvard. The range of his friendships, left-to-right, is recounted in chapter 5. Véliz photo.

5

The Friendships of Claudio Véliz

On an evening in April 1956, about the time a Soviet scuba diver was slitting the throat of an MI6 agent under the hull of the cruiser *Ordzhonikidze* in the Thames, Soviet leaders Nikita Khrushchev and Nikolai Bulganin were giving a reception at their Embassy in London. One of the guests was Claudio Véliz, then a twenty-five-year-old Ph.D. student at the London School of Economics. Khrushchev recognised him: "My *Chilean* friend!" he exclaimed in Russian, and then, through an interpreter, these words: "How good to see you again! Let me introduce you to Sir Anthony Eden and Lady Eden—and Charlie Chaplin!"

Khrushchev was not the first of Claudio's notable connections and far from the last. There have been hundreds around the world, many of them good friends, from half a dozen Nobel laureates (including Pablo Neruda) to American Supreme Court judges, from Margaret Thatcher to Salvador Allende and Ernesto (Che) Guevara. In his younger days Claudio was on the political left, but by the time I met him in 1981, in fact from the late 1960s, he had moved to a more right-populist position. His historical work is widely respected and frequently cited. More effectively than anyone else, he broke the reputation of Manning Clark in a single devastating 1982 article in *Quadrant* magazine titled "Bad History",[12] inevitably cited whenever Clark's posthumous reputation is seriously under discussion, while in another *Quadrant* article, which won the George Watson Prize for 1983, he pioneered the idea of a cultural "World Made in England".[13] Across the years he's talked to me about his experiences and connections. Some of it I taped.

I knew next to nothing about him until the southern autumn of 1981 when we first visited him and Maria Isabel Talavera Balmaceda at South Main, their ocean-front house directly below the Cinema Point lookout on Victoria's Great Ocean Road, ten kilometres north-east of Lorne. Kipling called the seaway past there "the great South Main" by analogy with the Spanish Main,[14] and the house had been given the name by a previous owner, Kathleen Fitzpatrick. I'd met them through my future wife Patricia,[15] a few months before our divorces came through and maybe six or seven months before our wedding, which they attended. On the strength of one conversation, he'd invited us down for dinner. I read up on him before driving there, even read his 1980 Clarendon Press volume, *The Centralist Tradition in Latin America.*[16]

I knew that in 1969 he'd been invited to Australia to deliver the Dyason Memorial Lectures, broadcast over the ABC.[17] Three years later

12 Claudio Véliz, "Bad History," *Quadrant*, 26, No. 5 (May 1982), 21–26.

13 Claudio Véliz, "A World Made in England," *Quadrant*, 27, No. 3 (March 1983), 8–19.

14 Rudyard Kipling, "The Flowers." Kipling visited Lorne in 1891.

15 Patricia Margarita San Martín, later (when I met her) Patricia Monypenny, then Patricia Ayres, a surname she still often uses along with Hübner, of Basque, Galician and northern Italian background, niece of Hernán San Martín Ferrari, Chilean ambassador to Zambia 1970–1973 and later of the Sorbonne—Claudio Véliz had met him more than once at Pablo Neruda's house in Isla Negra, Chile.

16 Claudio Véliz, *The Centralist Tradition in Latin America* (Clarendon Press, Oxford, 1980).

17 Claudio Véliz, "Centralism, Industrialization and Conformity in Latin America" and "Foreign Policy and the Rise of Nationalism in Latin America," publication of the Australian Institute of International Affairs (East Melbourne, 1969).

he had again come to Australia by invitation, this time to take up La Trobe University's Chair of Sociology. That was after his prestigious Institute of International Studies, founded by him at the University of Chile in 1966, was occupied by militants of the extreme-left *Movimiento de Izquierda Revolucionaria* (MIR, or Revolutionary Left Movement). All the Chileans I knew through Patricia had come to Australia to get away from the spiralling chaos of Salvador Allende's socialist revolution—mostly they were on the political right, though some were moderate Christian Democrats. All had left in 1971 or 1972 and most were in professions. Some returned to Chile after the 1973 *coup d'état*, against the flow of a contrasting political demographic getting out. When I married into the earlier category it included the Chilean consul in Melbourne, Eduardo Vives, who, along with Chile's Ambassador to Australia, Jorge Valdovino, was among our friends.

I remember as if it were last night the evening we first drove to South Main. There were heavy showers as we passed Fairhaven and Eastern View, along an undulating stretch of road with the hills coming up ahead and sheets of water slewing across the road. It was warm in the car and cold outside, the defrosting was minimal and I was wiping the glass with the back of my hand until Patricia passed me the pigskin gloves, her father's gloves. Every word and move had an intimate aspect and the relationship was still illicit. I'll omit the terms of endearment.

"Do you know much about their backgrounds?" I asked her at some point along that stretch. Not Claudio's, she told me, she knew little about him, but her parents knew Maria Isabel's family, south of Curicó, on their Viña Santa Lucía estate in the Central Valley. Like Patricia, Maria Isabel had attended a French school, but hers was in Paris. Later I learned that her Talavera roots went back to the conquistadors via Paraguayan *estancias* long since left. Maria Isabel's great uncle, José Manuel

Balmaceda, eleventh President of Chile, a reformer, had shot himself in the Argentine Embassy in Santiago after losing the Chilean civil war of 1891—instant sanctification in the eyes of his admirers. Claudio and Maria Isabel had children by previous marriages, and they had another house in Melbourne somewhere—Patricia had never been there, or to their place down here, so our curiosity was high. Subsequently we would spend lots of time with them.

The road began its circuitous ascent around Big Hill and after a couple of kilometres the look-out came into the headlights and passed us by on the left, just where the road swung right, a turn we didn't take—at that point we had to negotiate the precipitous descent on a rough track to the house. It took us three bites to get around a tight left turn, then another turn to the right further down, before we levelled out by the small cottage that had two more years to live before its consumption in the fires of Ash Wednesday, 1983, when many around there died. Subsequently it was rebuilt and expanded.

The showers had passed as suddenly as they'd hit. From below came the crashing of breakers on acres of rock-ledge. Everything smelled clean including the sour rot of eucalyptus leaves in the damp soil underfoot as we walked hand-in-hand to the door and the bell rigged-up there. Claudio welcomed us into the living room with its open fire. They're always playing opera tapes down there, so that would have been in the background. Maria Isabel was putting the finishing touches to the *hors d'oeuvres* and Claudio offered us drinks. Later we had dinner—possibly *empanadas* as an entrée and then a main course of *pastel de choclo* (beef and corn casserole) and salads. We often had those things there. Preserved fruits and ice cream typically followed, coffee and chocolates, and it was late when the two of us headed home to our upstairs flat on a hillside in the Melbourne suburb of Glen Iris.

I recall some of the conversation too. I brought up *The Centralist Tradition in Latin America* and Claudio talked about its distinction between the political tradition of Spain and Spanish America on the one hand (bureaucratic centralism, strong control from the metropolis) and, on the other, the freer individualistic Anglo-Saxon tradition. His analogy for the latter was the fox, for the former the hedgehog, a contrast later elaborated at length in *The New World of the Gothic Fox* (1994).[18] The fox knows many things in the way of survival, the hedgehog just one: extend spines. There was a dynamism to the Anglosphere, he argued, that enabled it to weather and master change better than the conservative, defensive, authoritarian Spanish Empire and its heirs.

So it was clear that he was an Anglophile, though his sensibilities were Continental and reflected an immersion in European philosophy and culture. Musically he was a Wagnerian. It was noticeable that his conversation never became argumentative. "You are *right*", he would say, "to a point", before patiently explaining how you were wrong. I liked the fact that he avoided moralising history, unlike many Marxists and some people on the right, the boring ones. He was interesting to look at, too. His beard and hair at that time were still predominantly dark, his eyes were animated and his voice engaging.

Over the years we've seen a great deal of each other. The Vélizes effectively supplemented my deceased parents in my affections, which is saying a lot. "I should put some of his experiences down on paper", I often thought, "because *he* won't, and all of those historical connections, places and scenes, they'll vanish with him. And to put it the right way around, *Khrushchev* knew *him*!"

18 Claudio Véliz, *The New World of the Gothic Fox: Culture and Economy in English and Spanish America* (University of California Press, Berkeley, Los Angeles, London, 1994).

Claudio Véliz Soza was born into one of Chile's oldest Presbyterian families, in a house on the Cerro Castillo in the coastal resort town of Viña del Mar, just north of the old port city of Valparaíso, on 21 July 1930. The summer palace of the President is on one side, private residences on the other. The President was General Carlos Ibáñez del Campo, who ruled by decree. To take the air, Claudio's mother would wheel him in his pram around the top of the hill and along the cliffs facing the Pacific, a stunning walk also enjoyed by one of Ibáñez's colleagues, Nelson Bravo, who would stop for a chat, and to pat the child on the head—its first political connection.

He was just two at the time of the farcical 100-day, *coup*-imposed Socialist Republic of Chile (June–September 1932), under Colonel Marmaduke Grove (both terminal *e*'s are sounded). One of its first acts was to order owners of pawnshops to return all merchandise to the owners free of charge—to the pawnbrokers' ruination.

His first sharp political memory is of the remarkable events surrounding the national elections of 1938. Just prior to those elections there was an attempted *coup d'état* by the *Movimiento Nacional Socialista de Chile*, the Chilean Nazi Party, principally consisting of university students. They intended, with the help of friends in the Army, to bring down the government of Arturo Alessandri and replace it with one led by Carlos Ibáñez, and to that end they took over the University buildings and the Workers' Insurance (*Securo Obrero*) building in front of the Government Palace.

"There was shooting left, right and centre", Claudio was saying as I pressed *Record*. "They expected—and they were deceived in this—that one of the military regiments would join them. The majority of them were hemmed in at the University of Chile and surrendered after a while—artillery was brought in and the great gates were shot down. The authorities took prisoners, sixty-odd students at the University, which is eight or so blocks from the Workers' Insurance building, one of the few skyscrapers in Santiago at the time, right by the Government Palace, where other students had made themselves strong on the top, from where they were shooting down. So these 60-odd students were marched down eight or ten blocks, hands up, to this building, and forced to walk upstairs ahead of the armed police as a shield so that the people up there couldn't shoot the police. The consequence was that the students on top of the building also surrendered. Then they took the lot, all these Nazi students, and lined them up in an alley or corridor, which is still there, right next to the building, and they shot them."

"No trial—nothing?" I asked.

"No, and this caused the most extraordinary revulsion throughout the country, a summary execution of all these students, however stupid they may have been, so there was a virtual rejection of the Alessandri regime—a liberal, moderate regime. To this day it's disputed who gave the order to shoot them. There's a bronze plaque there now, with their names."

"What happened next?"

"Something extraordinary. Ibáñez was the preferred candidate for the Nazis and fascistic people—he was not himself an extremist but a right-wing statist, believing social change lay in the direction of firm central control. When the shooting took place he was immediately arrested (though he claimed he had no advance knowledge of the attempted *coup*), and spent several days in jail. From jail he ordered his supporters, including the Nazi Party, to vote in favour of the left-wing Popular Front alliance, which, like the Popular Front alliance of France, had the moral support of the Comintern. So Chile is the only country in the world to have elected a Popular Front government with Nazi votes."

"But … the other parties?"

"I know, I know, you might think the Popular Front would have won anyway, but not at all. The Nazis had about 10,000 members so they certainly controlled at least that many votes. Their leader, Jorge González von Morées, transmitted to his followers Ibáñez's direction to vote for the Popular Front, which won by 4,000 votes, so if the Nazi Party hadn't supported them, the candidate of the right, Gustavo Ross (I was at school with his son), *he* would have won."

"You *knew* Ross?"

"I knew his son Jorge. So I was eight years of age when Chile came under the Popular Front, and I remember, distinctly, going down to a very beautiful square in Valparaíso called the Victory Square, and people marching around the square shouting slogans, and one of them, I still remember hearing it, was

El martillo, y la hoz,

mataran al chancho Ross!

('The hammer and the sickle will kill Ross the pig!')

"Anyway, the Popular Front won, and their leader, Pedro Aguirre Cerda, whom I never met—a Radical, an amiable and moderate Freemason (all Radicals were Freemasons)—he ruled throughout the War, during which Chile was neutral almost to the end."

"Like Sweden and Ireland, you had a *good* war?" I asked, "better than ours here."

"The war was something distant and entertaining", he laughed. "Every home had a map, and little pins, and, depending on where the battles were, you would move the pins around, and people would take bets—there was a sporting atmosphere about the war. In downtown

Santiago there was a cinema called *Principal*, which wasn't the principal cinema at all, just a little cinema to which you could go and watch, for an hour—any hour you liked—all the newsreels: the German *UFA* newsreel, the French *Pathé Journal* (the one with the cock), the American *Movietone*, and the British *Pathé*, all the newsreels at one sitting. Not everyone, however, felt neutral. Quite a few Chileans, people whose families had been there for generations, went to fight for the RAF, for the French, for the Wehrmacht."

By that time he was attending The Grange School, the prestigious English private boys' school in Santiago, having completed his elementary education at The Mackay School in Valparaíso. In class he sat next to young Carlos Kleiber, then exiled in South America with his father Erich. While at school Claudio won the cross-country and the two miles, his 400-metres freestyle record stood for a few years, and he took time to train with the Chilean Ski Team under Émile Allais, the great French alpine skier, who had established a skiing school in Chile.

At this stage he had two aspirations. His father, owner of the transport company *Expreso Universal*, was, among other things, a cattle importer and breeder of race horses, and the enthusiasm infected the son, whose principal ambition was to win the triple crown of the Chilean horse-racing calendar—the *Clásico El Ensayo*, the *Clásico St Leger*, and the Derby—with his own horse, bred and trained by himself. His second aspiration was to climb *Alto de los Leones*, 5380 metres and unconquered until 1939. In 1947 he won a Presidential (Pedro Aguirre Cerda) scholarship for entry to almost any university course he chose, and he chose animal husbandry at the University of Florida in Gainesville. There, he believed, he could learn to breed and train the greatest racehorse in Chilean history.

So in late August 1948, in company with a friend, he flew to Miami. On arrival at the airport they hailed a bus for the centre of town. The driver yanked the lever that opened the door and they entered, walking up to the long seat at the back so that they could sit together with their cases beside them. Other passengers, all black, entered along the route but remained standing, though there were plenty of empty seats. Finally the driver shouted back to Claudio and his friend, "Move to the *front,* or no one can *sit!*" It came as a shock that blacks could not sit in front of anyone white, and when, the following year, Councille Blye, an African-American, sought admission to the University, supported by the NAACP, Claudio joined the unsuccessful campaign to get him in. Years later Blye won admission and subsequently joined the Faculty, but controversy trailed him till his death on an undetermined date in January1983. His decomposed and mutilated body was found in a dumped refrigerator—drug deal gone wrong, apparently.

They travelled to Gainesville, a six-hour trip. Headlines in the papers featured Whittaker Chambers's latest revelations about Alger Hiss, and communist conspiracies were everywhere, none of which registered with the newcomers. Installed at the university, Claudio heard there were people offering odds of 50-to-1 that Dewey would beat Truman, so he bet all he could on a Truman victory, winning hundreds of dollars, and bought himself a car.

After a couple of terms he transferred from the B.A. course in animal husbandry to the B.Sc. course in agricultural economics, supplementing his minimal income by working as research assistant to Professor W. W. McPherson, who was investigating Chicago beef-market prices. After graduating B.Sc. in 1950, feeling he still knew nothing about economics, he applied for admission as a Ph.D. student at the London School of Economics and was subsequently accepted. Meanwhile in 1950 he had married Dorothy Ann Benson, an American graduate student from Toledo working at the University of Florida on symbolism in literature.

They had two children. She would later co-author a book on Cuba's national hero, José Martí, writer, patriot and anti-imperialist.

In September 1952 Claudio arrived in Britain. The mood in the new welfare state, co-endorsed by Churchill's ruling Conservatives, was bleak, reminiscent of *1984*, Orwell's numerical anagram for 1948. People were emigrating in droves, among them many doctors. Detector vans with electronic equipment prowled the streets in search of the 150,000 households committing the crime (*sic*) of having unlicensed television sets. Admitted homosexuals (Alan Turing, for instance, computer pioneer) were compulsorily treated with oestrogen or sent to jail. There was the odd liberal straw in the wind. At the LSE Michael Oakeshott had recently replaced the Marxist Harold Laski as Professor of Politics, to the dismay of the political left predominant there.

Claudio's supervisor was H. L. Beales, a Fabian socialist who had published on the industrial revolution and early British socialism.

"So, what do you wish to study, Mr Véliz?"

"The Theory of Value", Claudio replied.

"That's ridiculous!" Beales laughed. "Forget that. Study economic history, the real thing."

"Perhaps … the economic history of *Chile*?" Claudio tried.

"Ab-so-*lutely* ridiculous!" Beales replied. "Look, I'll lend you three books on the economic history of Britain. Read them, then come back with a sensible idea for a thesis." The result was a decision to examine the agricultural reform movement of the eighteenth century. Beales was delighted: "Now *that's* a subject!"

In addition to spending several years working in the British Museum Reading Room absorbed in the study of economic and social change, and attending seminars in sociology led by prominent scholars, Claudio was elected President of the Research Students Association, where his distinctive concept of the *Conversazione* was born. He initiated a series of Wednesday afternoon tea sessions in the Association's rooms, to which he invited one outside guest per week. Among them were extraordinary people, older types with established reputations such as the philosopher Bertrand Russell and Kingsley Martin, Editor of the *New Statesman and Nation*, as well as others whose careers lay ahead of them, for instance Paul Johnson (later editor of the same magazine) and Hugh Thomas, future historian and Labour candidate.

Around this time (1953–54) Claudio was elected Editor of the *Clare Market Review*, Britain's oldest student-run journal, published by the LSE Students' Union. He wrote articles for it, short stories and poems. It was announced that Isaiah Berlin would be visiting to deliver the annual Auguste Comte lecture on 12 May 1953. The lecture, "History as an Alibi", was subsequently published under the title "Historical Inevitability" and was an attack on that concept; thus it was implicitly anti-Marxist. Claudio had no intention of hearing a lecture by a right-winger, brilliant though he might be, and was walking away from the School when Dr Beales, coming in the opposite direction, asked "Aren't you going to the lecture?" and persuaded him to come along. The lecture infuriated Claudio because it appeared to undermine any possibility of social engineering. Accordingly he devoted a subsequent issue of the *Clare Market Review* (Lent, 1955) to an attack on Berlin after soliciting hostile articles including one by communist historian Eric Hobsbawm. Claudio's editorial was ferocious. "Today", he wrote, "we find ourselves in the midst of a revival of obscurantism; of a belief in man's incapacity to understand the causes and find the solutions of social problems", and that, he pointed out, went against the very purpose of the LSE. Surely there could be a real *science* of social change?—change underscored by belief in human improvability? It was appalling, he thought, that most young thinkers in Britain no longer accepted that. "The belief in man's capacity to solve problems of poverty, destitution and oppression through social policy is undermined by this new irrationalism", he lamented. By now Claudio was immersed in his Ph.D. on the enclosure movement and committed to political and social change, even revolutionary change, albeit through the ballot box. He says, however, that he never joined a political party.

Years later, in 1975, as Chairman of the Department of Sociology at LaTrobe University, he arranged for Isaiah Berlin to give guest lectures there. Berlin had kept a copy of the offending issue of the *Clare Market Review*, but now found Claudio agreeing with him. They became friends, meeting in Italy and the United States and attending the opera together at Covent Garden. Berlin was present at the launching of *The Centralist Tradition in Latin America*, and Claudio's subsequent book, *The New World of the Gothic Fox*, is dedicated to him.

Already by the mid-1950s Claudio was having second thoughts about at least some of his socialist assumptions. He had never been doctrinaire, and what he wrote in the early 1950s lacks the hard edge of dogma. His study of agrarian reform in the eighteenth century made him see that the common-field agriculture, destroyed by the enclosure movement, while perhaps it had entailed a happy way of life, nevertheless provided minimal productivity, bereft as it was of incentives and innovation. Its spirit of community was also its stranglehold.

And then there was the unedifying experience of being in at the gestation of what later became Amnesty International, and seeing at first hand how communists exploited people of good will in causes which, ostensibly noble, distorted complex political realities that he couldn't in all honesty ignore. As a child in Chile at the end of the 1930s he had got to know refugees from Franco's Spain, some of whom worked for his father as mechanics. A sympathetic listener, he later took up their cause in England, working for the International Brigades Association (IBA), whose members in London were mostly communists. As a Spanish-speaking Chilean postgraduate, too young to have been a combatant, he was an ideal courier and go-between, and on several trips to Spain from 1952 he liaised with lawyers and others trying to help political prisoners there. He has described the experience in his article "The True Genesis of Amnesty International" in a 2007 issue of *Quadrant*.[19] The communist head of the IBA in London, Alec Digges, was the man from whom Claudio took instructions for these trips and to whom he reported on return. In late November 1954, at the IBA's headquarters, Digges explained to Claudio and a non-communist friend, Peter Benenson (who in 1961 would formally convene Amnesty), his concept of such an organization, even suggesting the name "Amnesty". Digges, who had doubtless discussed the idea with the British Communist Party leadership, knew that to be effective it should not be headed by communists, just manipulated by them, and suggested Benenson head it. Benenson declined at that stage to be the front-man, or in Lenin's words the "useful idiot". Claudio also declined to be involved in any wider organization, which he thought premature in any case. By now he realised that the IBA and any new organisation it planned to promote would assist only communist prisoners. He'd tried to get it to help imprisoned Freemasons (Franco was intensely anti-Freemason), with only grudging co-operation.

Soon after arriving in England Claudio had been invited by Kingsley Martin, editor of *The New Statesman and Nation*, to write for him, but was also writing for the *Manchester Guardian*, *The Economist*, *Reynolds News*

19 *Quadrant*, 51, No. 5 (May 2007), 11–22.

(the co-operative movement's newspaper), the *Daily Herald* (Labour newspaper), and the *Daily Express*. One of the senior correspondents for the *Daily Express* was René McColl, who spent several months reporting from the Soviet Union in the early part of 1954. Claudio knew him.

Stalin had died on 5 March 1953, and Malenkov, the new Soviet leader, wished to promote an openness towards the West. In that context, the Soviet Embassy in London offered a free trip to the USSR for twenty British students, one from each of the major tertiary institutions. The applicant elected from the LSE was Claudio Véliz. Before leaving with the rest of the group, he ran into René McColl, who said he would get an introductory letter for Claudio to carry with him to someone of influence. A few days later the letter arrived, in a sealed envelope with a name written across the front in cyrillic. Claudio is not sure which of McColl's friends supplied it, but it may have been Cyrus Eaton or Armand Hammer, North American industrialists with business connections and powerful friends in the Soviet Union.

It was the spring of 1954, the month of May, and the majority of the party of twenty were in Leningrad. Among them was the young Harold Shukman, future historian and linguist. Some in the group had requested to meet with the great Russian poet Anna Akhmatova, publicly attacked in 1946 by Andrei Zhdanov who labelled her "part-whore, part-nun", "an overwought upper-class lady", "politically indifferent"—some high praise there. She had been expelled from the Writers' Union, though partially rehabilitated in 1951. A meeting, contrary to the visitors' expectations, was arranged, but Claudio was not there. He was in Moscow for an appointment of his own, staying at the Metropol, the grand Art Nouveau hotel built in Czarist times. In any case he had never heard of Akhmatova, so missing out on meeting with her in Leningrad meant nothing to him. Some days earlier he had shown the Intourist guide the envelope McColl had given him, and on seeing the name on the envelope her eyes had almost popped out of her head. An appointment had been arranged, and at the prescribed time an official car drew up outside the hotel.

Claudio was driven to an important civic building in central Moscow, not within the Kremlin itself, and escorted upstairs to a room with a large table on which sat a bottle of water and a couple of glasses. There was a wait of several minutes before Nikita Khrushchev entered with an interpreter, welcomed the visitor and invited him to sit. This man had worked very closely with Stalin, endorsing his policies and running the Ukraine for him, and you could say with justification that his political leadership was key to saving Stalingrad from surrender. Two years after Stalin's death, in February 1956, Khrushchev would be condemning him in the strongest terms in a secret speech to the Twentieth Congress of the CPSU. He had been foremost in organising the Politburo's ambush of Beria, his trial and execution—the last high Soviet official to suffer capital punishment and the most deserving.

"So, what are your impressions of the Soviet Union so far?" Khrushchev asked, smiling as he poured a glass of water for the visitor.

Well, Claudio's impressions were mostly positive, he replied, considering the devastation of the Great Patriotic War and how much that must have set things back, but he added that on the negative side, and given the homeless people he had seen on the streets, the lavishly-appointed Moscow Metro seemed an extravagance.

"I see your point, of course", Khrushchev replied, "but the way we see it, while the current generation may never experience a truly Communist society, at least while they're in the Metro they'll experience at first hand the world to which Communism aspires."

That was hard to contest. Khrushchev asked whether there was anything he could do to make Claudio's trip a success.

"I collect maps", Claudio told him, "—antique maps, and modern maps too. I've been up and down Gorky Street trying to find a good map of the Soviet Union, so far without success."

"That's no problem", Khrushchev replied. "Where are you staying?"

"The Metropol."

"Very well then, I'll have something delivered there in the next day", he promised, rising from his chair. The interview was over.

The following morning a long cardboard roll, wrapped and containing half a dozen maps of the Soviet Union, was delivered to the Metropol. The largest of these, displayed today at South Main, is printed on excellent paper, highly detailed, around two metres long and a metre high. Three of the six maps were destroyed in the Ash Wednesday fires of 1983 but not the largest, which at the time was in the Melbourne house.

When Khrushchev and Bulganin visited London in April 1956, Claudio received an invitation to the stand-up reception they held at the Soviet Embassy, and attended with Hugh Cudlipp, Editorial Director of the *Daily Mirror*. Having arrived at the Embassy they walked up the stairs to the greeting point, where Claudio was introduced as "Mr Claudio Véliz" and was at once recognised and embraced by Khrushchev, who then introduced him to Anthony and Clarissa Eden and Charlie Chaplin.

Later that year, his Ph.D. thesis not yet complete, Claudio returned to Chile on an invitation to edit Santiago's new morning tabloid *El Espectador*, in preparation for which he had been rotated through the various departments of Cudlipp's *Daily Mirror*, but he soon left *El Espectador* to take up the chair of economic history at the University of

Chile while continuing to write for the local press under the pseudonym Lautaro Fabian—particularly for the leftist evening paper *Las Noticias de Ultima Hora*, affiliated with the Socialist Party of Chile. Lautaro was the legendary sixteenth-century Mapuche leader who fought the Arauco War against the Spanish colonizers. "Fabian" signified faith in "the inevitability of gradualism", catch-cry of the British Fabian socialists, who shunned the path of violent revolution. Claudio was also writing for the monthly journal *Mensaje* published by the Jesuit *Centro Bellarmino*, and in 1957 organised the *Grupo Lautaro*, a Chilean Fabian society unrelated to the 1990s ultra-left underground group of that name.

In 1959 he was awarded the Ph.D. and the following year undertook archival work in London at the Public Record Office and the British Museum Reading Room for his first book, the history of the Chilean merchant marine,[20] a logical topic for someone who grew up around Valparaíso.

Then, from 1962 to 1966, he was Senior Research Fellow at the Royal Institute of International Affairs, Chatham House, where he organised regular seminars as well as a major conference on Latin America, editing the papers in two volumes, *Obstacles to Change in Latin America* and *The Politics of Conformity in Latin America.*[21] That conference was remarkable for its inclusion not only of academic historians and economists but industrialists, statesmen and financiers.

Among his closest friends through the 1960s was the Chilean poet and (later) Nobel laureate Pablo Neruda—there is a volume devoted to their correspondence.[22] Neruda was a prominent member of

20 *Historia de la marina mercante de Chile* (University of Chile Press, Santiago, 1961).

21 Claudio Véliz, *Obstacles to Change in Latin America* and *The Politics of Conformity in Latin America* (Oxford University Press, 1965 and 1967). These were followed a year later by *Latin America and the Caribbean: A Handbook* (Fredrick A. Praeger, London, 1968).

22 *Pablo Neruda–Claudio Véliz, correspondencia en el camino al Premio Nóbel, 1963–1970*, ed. Abraham Quezada Vergara, *Fuentes para la historia de la república*, XXXIV (Dirección de Bibliotecas, Archivios y Museos, Santiago de Chile, 2011).

the Chilean Communist Party and a person of wide sympathies and profound humanity. Their letters reflect their mutual affection and their contemporary attitudes.

In 1963 Claudio visited Cuba with a small group of Chilean economists drawn from the Lautaro Group, including Jaime Barrios (who later headed Banco Central under Allende's *Unidad Popular* (UP) Government, was in the Moneda Palace with Allende on 11 September 1973 when it was under air attack, and disappeared a couple of days later, presumably executed), Alban Lataste Hoffer (later author of a book on the Cuban economy), and Sergio and German Aranda. They were invited by Carlos Rafael Rodríguez, Secretary-General of the Cuban Communist Party and head of the National Institute of Agrarian Reform, and Ernesto Che Guevara, to stay and help manage various aspects of the Cuban economy. Knowing Rodríguez's weakness for Stilton cheese, Claudio would later send him Stiltons in small china jars purchased at the famous Paxton & Whitfield cheese shop in Jermyn Street, via friends who happened to be travelling from England or the Continent to Cuba—friends like Richard Gott, who mentions this in the Prologue to his history of Cuba.[23]

Che Guevara welcomed the group at an informal meeting in Havana.

"What did he say?" I asked.

"He had immense presence and great charm, and he said to us (I remember it clearly), 'We want you to join us. Stay with us, work with us, help us to strengthen the economic foundations here, help the revolution to prosper, and make the future *work*.'"

"So you got to know Che?"

23 Richard Gott, *Cuba: A New History* (Yale University Press, New Haven, 2004).

"Well, I knew him well enough to commission him to write an article for *International Affairs*, the Chatham House journal, on the Cuban economy. It appeared in volume 40 if I recall, in late 1964."[24]

I asked Claudio for his impressions of Fidel Castro.

"We were at this enormous rally in Havana", Claudio recalled, "it was the 26th of July, 1963, and I was sitting directly below Fidel. He was up on the tribunal, the rostrum, addressing a vast crowd, a million people. It was the tenth anniversary of his failed attack on the Moncada barracks, which was the start of the revolution that culminated six years later with the entry of his columns into Havana on the night of 31 December 1958. He spoke for six hours and I took many photographs, all destroyed at South Main in the fire of '83. He is—or he was—a tremendous orator, and would keep the people entertained, peppering his address with intermissions: 'This is a good time for exercise: let's dance to "Guantanamera"'; or 'We'll take a fifteen-minute break for those who need to go to the latrines'. It was marvellous spectacle."

All except Claudio stayed on, serving at senior levels of the revolutionary government for several years. Claudio declined because, he says, "I felt professionally inadequate, and mainly because I found the climate intolerable." While in Cuba he met and befriended the Polish artist Feliks Topolski and wrote the accompanying text for Topolski's illustrations ("Chronicle") of Castro's Cuba.[25] This essay covered the achievements and failures of the Cuban revolution as Claudio saw them shortly after the October 1962 Cuban missile crisis. In the six decades following its independence from Spain, Cuba was a cultural vacuum filled from Miami "with all the things U.S. tourists love to enjoy anonymously and away from home"—one of the best sentences in the

24 Ernesto Che Guevara, "The Cuban Economy: Its Past and Its Present Importance," *International Affairs*, 40, No. 4 (October 1964).

25 Claudio Véliz, "Cuba," in Feliks Topolski, *Chronicle* 17–20 [245–248], Vol. XI, 1963.

piece. "Havana became a gigantic brothel", he went on, "and gambling den for the millions who could not afford a return flight elsewhere. The worst elements of U.S. culture crawled south and found their way into the island"—a "moral and cultural annihilation". The revolution of 1959 was a rejection of all that. In its place was "the enthusiastic, naïve, dynamic and almost childish energy with which a people go about the task of filling a cultural vacuum from within". The revolution was national well before it ever called itself communist, indeed it remained essentially national, refusing to borrow culturally from China or the USSR (he made the same point to Neruda in a contemporary letter: "*lo importante de la revolución cubana es precisamente su latinoamericanismo*," "the importance of the Cuban revolution is precisely its Latin American nature")[26]. In remaking itself, he pointed out, the revolution made mistakes, including the imposition of equal wages. On landed estates and sugar plantations the government encouraged autonomous co-operatives, a fiasco soon replaced by state-run farms. Most foods and almost all consumer goods had been imported from the United States, a "parasitic dependence", so that when that country blockaded the island severe shortages were inevitable. Everything was rationed, though the rationing schedules, on the whole, were generous. Attempting to diversify Cuba's economy, the revolution had slashed the size of the sugar plantations, with disastrous results prompting an abrupt about-turn. The same was true of industrial policy. There was little discontent, though, amid the exigencies of a war economy triggered by the Bay of Pigs affair and the missile crisis, through both of which Cuba had emerged victorious, refusing America's demands for inspections and shooting down a U2 spy plane, which Claudio had viewed at Havana's Revolutionary Museum. "Of course we won", Cubans would say to him. "If we had lost we wouldn't be here, would we?"

26 Claudio Véliz to Pablo Neruda, 14 August 1963, in *Pablo Neruda–Claudio Véliz, correspondencia en el camino al Premio Nóbel, 1963–1970*, p. 53.

In 1966 Claudio approached the Rector of the University of Chile, Eugenio González Rojas, with a proposal: set up an overtly elitist Institute of International Studies within the university, at postgraduate level, along the lines of Chatham House, and directly under the Rector—no connection with any of the faculties. The Institute, he argued, should be a forum for the free expression of views, a sanctuary, its members meeting regularly for dinner—which should be a good dinner—around a high table of the Oxbridge variety with invited guests, local and overseas, a place where astronomers could meet historians, academics mingle with businessmen and politicians. González accepted the idea in its entirety and proceeded to set it up under Claudio's directorship, giving him a free hand. The guiding principle of its seminars was derived from Michael Oakeshott:

> The pursuit of learning is not a race in which the competitors jockey for the best place, it is not even an argument or a symposium; it is a conversation. ... A conversation does not need a chairman, it has no predetermined course, we do not ask what it is 'for', and we do not judge its excellence by its conclusions; it has no conclusion, but is always put by for another day. Its integration is not superimposed but springs from the quality of the voices which speak, and its value lies in the relics it leaves behind in the minds of those who participate.[27]

Claudio appointed, as the academic core, five research professors: John Gittings, Richard Gott, Alain Joxe (all from Chatham House), Marcos Kaplan, and Osvaldo Sunkel. Gittings was an historian interested in Mao's China and the People's Liberation Army, later senior editor and writer with *The Guardian*. Gott was a left-wing historian who started his book on Latin American guerrilla movements while he was at the Institute; later literary editor for *The Guardian*, he resigned when it was revealed that he had accepted money from the KGB. Alain Joxe,

27 Michael Oakeshott, *The Voice of Liberal Learning*, ed. Timothy Fuller (Yale University Press, New Haven, 1989).

sociologist and historian, was the son of Louis Joxe, minister under General de Gaulle, but Alain was far to the left of Gaullism; he still writes—his anti-globalist *Empire of Disorder* was published in 2002, a title whose vindication has well and truly arrived.[28] Kaplan was an Argentine sociologist, Sunkel a Chilean economic historian. In addition there were associates in Argentina, Brazil and the United States. "I recall that [Claudio] had enemies in the university, and outside too, who made his life more difficult", John Gittings told me; however, "with his unfailing optimism and conviction he could work around such difficulties". Later, at La Trobe University in Melbourne, he would face similar hostility to his evening and weekend *Conversazioni*, decried by some colleagues as elitist.

Claudio thinks Richard Gott one of the most interesting of those he appointed.

"Interesting *how*?" I asked.

"In more ways than one—I'll give an example. Like me, Gott had met Che in Cuba. Che was enormously charming, hugely charismatic, and Richard immediately liked him. Anyway, in 1967 Richard decided, without consulting me, to try to meet up with him in neighbouring Bolivia, where Che was leading a hopeless insurgency. Some time in 1967, perhaps late September, Richard asked me if he could have a few weeks' leave to drive to Buenos Aires. I said 'OK'. Some weeks later it was announced that Richard had identified Che's corpse in Bolivia, several hours after his execution. The CIA were involved. As one of only two people in the vicinity who had met Che, Richard was qualified to identify him.

"Anyway, time went by, and then I was called into the Moneda [the Presidential Palace] by President Frei's Minister for Foreign Affairs, Gabriel Valdés, who told me 'Look, you have this gringo working for

28 Alain Joxe, *Empire of Disorder* (Semiotext(e), New York, 2002).

you—Gott. We don't want him here. Get rid of him. Get rid of this bastard.'

"I told him, 'I can't just sack him, and I don't want to get rid of him.' Valdés was furious: 'You get him out, or I will!' Months went by, and nothing happened. Perhaps the CIA were pressuring Valdés."

When Claudio advertised for a personal assistant around this time, one of the applicants turned out to be Maria Isabel Talavera, who was looking for an interesting part-time job, and certainly not for the turning-point it was. She'd lived a contented and comfortable family life until the moment she sat down in that office.

Claudio maintains that the political alignment of his Institute was perceived as neutral, but in the view of people with whom I spoke in Chile in 1982 and 1985 it was certainly leftist, not centrist. However, it would be fair to call it neutral as between President Eduardo Frei's left–reformist "Revolution in Freedom" and the opposition Socialist/UP's Marxist line. The Institute's regular guests included President Frei, Socialist Party and UP leader Salvador Allende and his deputy, Senator Carlos Altamirano, Pablo Neruda, and Commanders-in-Chief of the Army General René Schneider, a strong constitutionalist (murdered in 1970 by right-wing extremists) and General Carlos Prats (assassinated by the Chilean DINA security agency in Argentina in 1974). With all these people Claudio was on good terms, and they returned his hospitality.

From overseas, too, he brought many significant guest lecturers. They included Kenneth Younger, Director of the Royal Institute of International Affairs and formerly Britain's Acting Foreign Secretary during Ernest Bevin's protracted illness, Andrew Schonfield, the Royal Institute's director of research (and economics editor of *The Observer*), and the historian Arnold Toynbee.

On Younger's arrival, John Gittings told me, "Claudio asked him 'How are things in Europe, Kenneth?' to which Younger replied 'I don't know; I haven't been there for several months'. Claudio had to struggle to hide his amazement that the director of *the* British Institute of International Affairs in the modern age should not regard Britain as part of Europe."

Toynbee, whom Claudio had known from his days at the LSE, was fascinated by the Inca Empire and had recently written the Foreword to Harold V. Livermore's translation of Garcilaso de la Vega.[29] Toynbee's theory of civilisational rise and collapse turned on challenge and response, and he liked to visit the scenes of historical conflicts, seeing and touching them for himself. His visit to the Institute, at which he was to speak about contemporary history, came with a request—take him to the southern-most extent of the Inca Empire, along the River Maule that flows from the Andes to the Pacific Ocean just north of Constitución in south-central Chile. There, where there are still Inca mummies buried on the hilltops, the legend goes that in the 1490s an army of Mapuche Indians stopped the Incas' southward advance—although in the view of some Chilean historians, including Claudio, the Incas reached even further south, to the latitude of the island of Chiloé.

Claudio's old schoolmate Jorge Ross (son of Gustavo Ross) had a six-seater plane and a very good pilot, and agreed to fly Toynbee and Claudio over the length of the Maule. They were joined by Agustín Edwards, owner of Chile's largest newspaper, the conservative *El Mercurio.* Claudio knew him from schooldays at The Grange. After a spectacular flight under blue skies, from one Andean peak to another, intermittently circling the craters of active volcanoes and then straight down to the mouth of the river for a low-level circuit of the putative

[29] Garcilaso de la Vega, *Royal Commentaries of the Incas and General History of Peru* (University of Texas Press, 1966).

battle-ground, they stayed at Edwards's *fundo* or ranch between Temuco and the Andes. A few days later they flew north, up along the Andes and then west to La Serena, from where it's an easy drive to the Valle del Encanto to inspect the rock art of the Diaguita and Molle peoples, a culture destroyed in the Incan advance of the 1490s. These were the most spectacular site-inspections Toynbee had ever undertaken and he said so.

Though he was not a member of Chile's Socialist Party, Claudio had been a friend of Salvador Allende and his family for years. He had stayed with them in Chile and entertained them in London, introducing Señora Hortensia Allende to Bertrand Russell, for example. He had helped Allende by way of articles and the writing of speeches. But when Allende returned to Chile from one of his trips to Cuba in the mid-1960s he seemed a changed man. That was obvious at a dinner party Claudio attended at Allende's Santiago house.

"He said to his family, he said to me, that he had had a life-changing experience in Cuba. He had stood with Fidel in Havana in front of a million people, 'an ocean of people' were his words, and after Fidel introduced him the crowd chanted 'A-yen-day A-yen-day, A-yen-day' many times over. Salvador Allende, one-time President of the Chilean Senate, had been a punctilious constitutionalist all the way back to 1938 when he was Minister for Health in the Popular Front government of Pedro Aguirre Cerda. Now he was questioning himself on that very constitutionality. Parliamentary democracy in Chile, he was saying, amounted to a frustrating process for change; Cuba, by contrast, had taken a much-needed short-cut."

Claudio thought this a false dilemma, at the time and now. Chile was not Cuba. While he accepted that Attaturk, for example, could not in a democratic way have achieved what he did, that was because of the conditions at the end of the Ottoman Empire—the only viable way was authoritarian if one were to use power in order to modernise. But in Chile the parliamentary way was deeply enshrined.

They had neighbouring seaside homes, and during a long walk on the beach in the lead-up to the 1970 elections that gave Allende power, Claudio wished him well but told him he did not feel able to help him this time around. He would not criticise him, but simply "stay at home" and concentrate on a major conference he was organising, the *Conferencia del Pacífico* (27 September–3 October 1970). On 4 September Allende won the Presidential election with a plurality of 36.2 per cent of the votes, and over the next two months there were negotiations between Congress, Allende's Popular Unity and the Christian Democrats over the formation of a government, leading to Allende's accession to real power on 3 November 1970. In a cordial letter to Pablo Neruda written that night from London, Claudio welcomed "*una nueva era en la historia política de Chile*", refraining from expressing doubts that by then were dominating his mind.[30] In the two months between the elections and Allende's assumption of power Claudio presided over his Conference of the Pacific in Viña del Mar, which for the first time brought together speakers from all major states of the Pacific rim "to intensify research on the natural, scientific, socio-economical, historical, legal, cultural and technological aspects of the Pacific Ocean."[31]

From late 1970 Chile's political tensions were beginning their long spiral out of control. Already by the time of the Conference of the Pacific things at the University of Chile had begun to change in interesting

30 Claudio Véliz to Pablo Neruda, 3 November 1970, in *Pablo Neruda–Claudio Véliz, correspondencia en el camino al Premio Nóbel, 1963–1970*, p. 159.

31 *Centro de estudios del Pacífico* (Valparaíso, 1971), "Background", p. 5. There was an article on the conference in the Chilean weekly *Ercilla*, No. 1841, 30 September–6 October 1970, "Mare Nostrum del siglo XXI," pp. 45–56, and in the major newspapers of Santiago and Valparaíso of the time.

ways. There was a movement from within Claudio's Institute, led by people he had himself appointed, to "democratise" it, and (in their own terms) transform it into a vanguard, or "forward trench in the struggle against Imperialism". Some thought everyone there should have one vote at staff meetings, even the janitor; as for the Director, he should be elected by direct vote of the members. Claudio point-blank refused to compromise, so in practical terms the Institute was now fractured. These people were not communists. The Chilean communists within Popular Unity, in fact most Latin American communists apart from a few like Che Guevara, were relatively conservative Moscow-leaning people who believed, at least ostensibly, in working within constitutional structures. They were not Trotskyists (that is, permanent-revolutionists, world-revolutionists). Their slogan from 1972 was "Consolidate to Advance", directed against extra-legal, chaos-creating actions of the far-left. But the radicals in Claudio's Institute (and he was not letting go of it) were hot-headed revolutionaries of the MIR persuasion, well to the left of Popular Unity, which they wished to push into more and more extreme courses. Some of them were very small-minded for members of an institute of international studies, apparently unaware of new currents of Marxism in the United States. They vetoed, for example, Claudio's invitation to Herbert Marcuse, issued personally at the University of California San Diego, to visit the Institute—an invitation Marcuse had accepted. They'd never heard of him ("some Yanqui").

Following on from the Pacific Conference, the Institute needed funds from various bodies to recoup travel expenses and honoraria. Disbursements were made in US dollars. For this, Claudio was not only criticised by some of his colleagues, one of them reported him to the police. At 4.00 a.m. there was a knock on the door of his flat, he was arrested on the spot and taken in for interrogation. His friends got the lawyer Miguel Schweitzer (later a minister and ambassador) to help, even got Allende to help, and by evening Claudio was released.

And then one night the *MIRistas* took over the Institute entirely. When Claudio arrived the next morning there were red flags and banners draped all over, and the slogan "Transforming this institute into a forward trench against imperialism". He was forbidden to enter. This was not an act of the Allende government, which was losing control of events, but an unapproved *ad hoc* takeover (*toma*) by extremists. The historian Hugh Thomas arrived to present a seminar paper and Claudio had to arrange for him to speak in a downtown building, the premises of the Council of University Rectors, where the Institute continued to conduct occasional seminars.

Opposing demonstrations by the left and right were an almost daily affair and everyone in the city knew what teargas smelt like. Through 1971 and 1972 the end of all this was increasingly predictable, and by many desired. There were not just the arbitrary, extra-legal *tomas* of farms but killings of the owners of those farms, expropriations of factories, crumbling social structures. It's repeatedly claimed by the left that the Chilean armed forces were pushed into the *coup* by the Nixon administration, but in the circumstances of growing anarchy no pushing was required. Slogans urging it began to appear on walls ("Jakarta is coming"), while out at the military academy young women from the Christian Democratic right and more radical-right groupings like *Patria y Libertad* would gather to throw wheat over the perimeter at the officers inside, calling "Here, chickens, chickens!"—provocation in mini-skirts, sexually charged. I had this first-hand from Patricia. Of course the economic chaos was in some part the result of United States embargoes, intended to this end. It also has to be said that many initiatives of the Allende government were good for Chile and were not reversed by the Pinochet government—most of the redistribution of land including many forced *tomas* was left in place. But the country was sick with politics, paralysed.

News of the takeover of the Institute had reached Australia, and Claudio's friends there were concerned—people like Heinz Arndt and Oscar Spate at the ANU, and Bruce Grant (all three had spoken at the Pacific Conference in Viña del Mar). Spate wrote asking whether Claudio would be interested in a chair of sociology at the new La Trobe University in Melbourne—Spate said he would ask La Trobe to write with details. Essentially, it was an invitation. Claudio, however, had never studied sociology. He had read in it—who hadn't?—but he had no qualifications, so he wrote back with what he intended as a polite "No" which was interpreted as "I will give the matter further consideration". This was late-1971. Three months later a telephone call came from La Trobe's Registrar: how long before a firm decision? Airline tickets were offered for a visit to look over the university and Claudio accepted, coming across with Maria Isabel.

A couple of months later he telephoned David Myers, vice-chancellor at La Trobe, asking what would be the minimum period he might with decorum serve in the position. Myers thought less than three years would be unusual. So Claudio and Maria Isabel held a meeting with her children and talked about the beautiful countryside, the surfing, the skiing and the kangaroos, and the idea was accepted. They also brought one maid with them.

Meanwhile the occupiers of the Institute had broken into Claudio's files, destroying or stealing all his correspondence with Allende, much of his correspondence with Neruda, and many of the papers from the Pacific Conference, along with everything else there. Effectively the place had ceased to function. Following the *coup* of 11 September 1973, by which time he had long since left, it was delivered from the hands of its occupiers who, terrified at the prospect of real bullets, fled their forward trench. The Institute was soon its old self again thanks to good leadership and a renewed obsession with academic excellence—over half a dozen Chilean ambassadors were among its graduates. A second Pacific Conference was organised for 1979.

During his Institute's long occupation Claudio saw a lot of Neruda, who was appalled at the takeover and offered to speak out in support. "The best way," Claudio told him, "is to do and say nothing." Of course Neruda was totally committed to Allende, as his 1972 collection of poetry, *A Call for Nixon-icide and Praise for the Chilean Revolution*, shows,[32] but he had little more time for the wreckers on the ultra-left than he had for Nixon and Kissinger. As for Claudio, his political attitudes were rapidly transforming, though his friendship with Neruda (who had not long to live) was above politics. Recent experiences had been distressing and everything needed re-thinking, including the relationship of institutes like his to the universities of which they were part. If they were vulnerable to takeovers in times of political turmoil, perhaps their proceedings should somehow be distinguished from the academy, or even private.

It was at La Trobe University that Claudio created the occasional "*Conversazione* on Culture and Society", modelled on the seminars he had run at his Institute in Chile and at Chatham House. They took place within the university but were not predominantly *of* the university. Speakers and audiences came mostly from outside—from the worlds of politics, business, diplomacy, the press, the arts, religion—though a few members of faculty would come along too. Attendance was by invitation, the lists of participants constantly changing at this time,

32 Pablo Neruda, *Incitación al Nixonicidio y alabanza de la revolución chilena* (Editorial Causachun, Lima, 1973).

though retaining a stable core to provide an institutional memory.

In October of 1988 he ran a three-day *Conversazione* on "The Idea of a University" including an introductory reception, two dinners and two luncheons. This was as impressive as any such event he had organised at Chatham House or the University of Chile. The speakers were Sir Claus Moser, Warden of Wadham College Oxford; the historian Sheldon Rothblatt from the University of California at Berkeley; John Silber, President of Boston University; David Caro, former Vice Chancellor of the University of Melbourne; Sir Alan Peacock, former Vice Chancellor of the University of Buckingham; Sir Bruce Williams, former Vice Chancellor of the University of Sydney; and Dame Leonie Kramer from the University of Sydney. Perhaps the most interesting of these was the ruthless and successful John Silber, who had pulled Boston University (originally a small Methodist institution, and now one of the largest private universities in America) from its very mediocre ratings up into America's top twenty, a stunning achievement.

Towards the end of the weekend *Conversazione* Silber took Claudio aside for a long talk. He admitted he had never before heard of this place. Claudio said he wasn't surprised—La Trobe University was entirely off the radar for most guests at these *Conversazioni.*

In that respect, Silber replied, it was like Boston University. Everyone had heard of Harvard and MIT, few of Boston University. He'd been trying to rectify that, and had set up a "university within the university" that he titled "The University Professors Program", appointing outstanding scholars including Nobel Prize winners, and paying them considerably more than he was paying the rest of the university's full professors. Many in his university, he admitted, hated him for that, as well as other things, but he was there to lead, not defer to committees. Would Claudio be willing to come to BU for a few months the following year, 1989, the university's sesquicentenary, and organise a celebratory *Conversazione* on any topic he liked?

Claudio took leave from La Trobe for the interim and I agreed to look after South Main. In Boston he organised a major *Conversazione* on the theme "A Metaphor for Our Times" (18–19 September 1989). Speakers came from within the United States (Arthur Schlesinger and Walt Rostow), from Britain (Hugh Thomas, Bernard Levin and Ernest Gellner), from France (Emmanuel Le Roy Ladourie and Cornelius Castoriadis), and from Australia (Leonie Kramer and Claudio himself).

Silber, who chaired some of the sessions, had been encouraging Claudio to develop a tripartite series of rolling *Conversazioni* involving triennial sessions at each of Boston University, Wadham College Oxford (the Claus Moser connection) and La Trobe University in Melbourne (other Oxford colleges, Lincoln and Magdalen, came in later); this 1989 Boston *Conversazione* was in fact the first of these.

Following this event, over lunch at the Algonquin Club, on Commonwealth Avenue, Silber made an offer: "I want you to stay, and I want you to be our dean of Arts". This would have involved much administration and fund-raising (not Claudio's strengths), so on that ground he declined. Silber then said "I've got a better idea: run the University Professors Program", and Claudio accepted on the spot. This would also enable him to organise, in addition to the rolling Boston–Oxford–Melbourne *Conversazioni*, a regular series of local *Conversazioni* under the auspices of the University Professors, four a year, attracting high-profile international speakers to help put BU on the map—at least for those speakers, who would spread the word. And he would have a chair of history into the bargain, and be on the Council of Deans. The arrangement lasted thirteen years from 1990 to 2003, when he retired at the age of 73.

As Silber's baby the University Professors section was highly privileged. Admission to its programs depended on SAT scores around the 1400 level, and it granted its own interdisciplinary degrees. Only the brightest BU students were accepted. I taught with the University Professors through 2001 so I have direct knowledge of it. The students loved it because they were made to feel special. They were even better than the students I'd taught at Vassar College in 1993, which is saying something. There were 34 attached scholars and a student body of just 124 undergraduates but 36 doctoral candidates in 2002/2003. Its faculty at that time included three Nobel Prize winners (Sheldon Glashow, Elie Wiesel and Saul Bellow) and the brilliant English poet Geoffrey Hill. The *Conversazioni* organised under its auspices included among the speakers Stephen Breyer of the US Supreme Court, the Nobel Prize-winning writer Mario Vargas Llosa, historians Alan Bullock, Hugh Thomas, Richard Pipes and Francis Fukuyama, literary critic Christopher Ricks, academic lawyer Alan Dershowitz, sociologist Peter Berger, conductor Christopher Hogwood, and many others of equal calibre.

Members of the University Professors I met all appreciated the way Claudio ran the show, and people in other departments of the university to whom I spoke, who had addressed some of the many *Conversazioni* he organised, thought he handled the job well. That included Christopher Ricks, too intelligent and abrasively witty to be tolerated by the perverse English Department, which had blackballed Geoffrey Hill (I'm not making that up). Ricks had moved sideways and formed "The Republic of Letters" with Bellow and Hill. I liked and admired Ricks and his work—except maybe his book on Bob Dylan, though that has its good bits—and I lunched with him on several occasions. He told me he didn't much like Claudio, but then added "he's a brilliant impresario".

For most of her beneficiaries Fortune's ultimately a wrecker. In

2003, the same year Claudio left Boston University, John Silber retired from the Chancellorship and Interim Presidency. Almost at once his enemies struck at his key legacies. Within a year Boston dropped out of the tripartite *Conversazione* arrangement. There was a short-lived attempt to replace it with *Conversazioni* at the University of Vancouver but only one was ever held there, relegated by the authorities to an inappropriate facility. BU's University Professors section, perhaps Silber's proudest achievement, was phased out from 2009 and ceased to exist in 2011. Its enemies claimed it sent the wrong message, that its very excellence devalued the other 95 per cent of the university. Thus from 2004 the *Conversazione* existed only in the city of Melbourne, its activities overseen by its Melbourne Committee, which continued to organise one or two *Conversazioni* each year on important topics with notable speakers. Venues were all within the central business district. Without a doubt the most impressive of these was that held on 22 and 23 October 2005 on "Judicial Activism: Power Without Responsibility?" The audiences were refreshingly younger than they often have been. Two of the nine US Supreme Court justices, Stephen Breyer and Antonin Scalia, were among the speakers, who included Justices Dyson Heydon and Michael Kirby of the High Court of Australia, historian Andrew Roberts, writer Renata Adler, journalist Melanie Phillips, and academic lawyer Michael Coper. *Conversazioni*, one or two a year organised by Claudio, continue in Melbourne to this day.

From the outset, for Claudio Véliz, history was something lived, with affective affinities running left-to-right, and he's disinclined to repudiate any part of his past. Opinions shift with experience, but one's varying directions in politics and life are choices on a continuum, each valid and perhaps inevitable in context. The one person signs off on it all.

Diana Mitford, later Diana Mosley. Chatsworth connection and correspondent. "I thought the bomb plot despicable." Getty Images.

6

Things Diana Mosley Told Me

I was working at Chatsworth House in Derbyshire for a few weeks in the early spring of 1990, having flown across from Virginia after staying with friends on the eastern shore of Chesapeake Bay. Chatsworth is the home of the Dukes of Devonshire and a large part of it is open to the public most days. I was there to carry out the first descriptive analysis of the eighteenth-century library of Lord Burlington, the neo-Palladian architect earl. This work materialised as "Burlington's Library at Chiswick", published in the leading journal in its field, *Studies in Bibliography* (University of Virginia); later it formed a part of my book on classicism and culture in eighteenth-century England, published by Cambridge University Press in 1997. A generation after Burlington died his library was transferred from his London home, Chiswick Villa, to Chatsworth as a result of a marriage joining the two families, and has remained part of the Chatsworth library ever since.

Renting a car at Heathrow, I drove directly up to Bakewell, a couple of miles from Chatsworth, paid for a three-week stay at a homely bed-and-breakfast place I'd booked from America, hung my clothes in the closet and drove across the hill through the mist and drizzle and on down to the big house. It was freezing cold and there were just one or two cars in the parking lot, with no one walking about. A few of the trees were coming into leaf but most were bare.

If you're carrying out research there you first register and then they show you to a room in the basement. The books or manuscripts you wish to consult are brought down to you. No one works in the library itself, which is up on the second storey, part of the tour of the house (visitors can look into but not walk into it). They gave me Burlington's 1743 library catalogue to work from, and by using that I could ask to see any of the books it listed, but it was impractical to make an efficient study of Burlington's library from the basement.

On the second day the Duchess of Devonshire came down with an assistant to make photocopies and spoke to me. She asked what I was working on and where I came from. I told her and she said "Well, you must stay with us, then". Unfortunately I was committed to staying in town. When I explained to the Duchess that I was preparing a detailed descriptive analysis of Lord Burlington's library from his 1743 catalogue and the books themselves, she arranged for me to work up in the library instead of down in the basement. I was told by the curator that it was the first time in ages that any visitor had worked up there, among the exquisite bookcases and desks including one that was Burlington's own. I worked at that desk with the books from his Chiswick library all around me. It was the most enjoyable project I've ever undertaken and I felt as if Burlington were present. I could examine the entire range of his books, write all my notes about them at his desk, and photograph examples of his bespoke bindings. Visitors would peer in: "Somebody's *reading* in there!"

Taking an hour or more off for lunch, I'd go down and buy sandwiches to eat in the gardens, exploring the rhododendron walk, the yew maze, the riverbank and the deer park. I'd also flip through the books they had for sale.

There were several books about the Mitford sisters. One of those sisters was Deborah Mitford, now the Duchess of Devonshire and mistress of Chatsworth, whom I'd just met. I knew something about a couple of the others from their books, or from books about them (like David Pryce-Jones's book on Unity Mitford), but I didn't know much about the one whose pictures took my eye, Diana Mitford, later Diana Guinness, subsequently Diana Mosley, married to Sir Oswald Mosley, capital-L Leader of the British Union of Fascists during the 1930s. She'd been described as "the most beautiful woman in the world". I was attracted by her looks and of course her notoriety.

Between periods of research I started reading about the Mosleys and their attachment to Fascism, particularly *via* the pages of Lady Mosley's autobiography *A Life of Contrasts*. Like her sister Unity, Diana Mosley was frequently in Germany. Hitler was a witness at her wedding to Sir Oswald. She and Mosley were also close friends with the Goerings and the Goebbels. This was the Paris-based sister of the woman who was facilitating my work in the Chatsworth library.

I was thinking about this side-reading while photographing the Burlington bindings. Lord Burlington was a man of impeccable and studied taste in every detail of his life and work, from the houses he designed to the bespoke mathematical instruments he used to design them, and one expects and finds a classical elegance in the bindings of his books. His binder was Thomas Elliott, who also worked for the Harleian Library. Burlington's library was rich in the works of Italian architects of the sixteenth century, pre-eminently Andrea Palladio. Like the Mosleys he loved Italy, where he'd familiarised himself with the architecture of the *cinquecento* and established powerful connections among the aristocracy and the *cognoscenti*. He was looking to recreate in England an architectural aesthetic that would reanimate something of Roman Britain, suitably updated and inspired by Palladio's sixteenth-century architectural work around Vicenza. Oswald Mosley's take on Fascism was a down-market equivalent, an attempted transplantation to Britain of Mussolini's quest for a Futurist *romanità*, a reanimation of Roman-ness based on the order and authority represented by the *fasces*, the rods and axes of authority unbreakably united by leather bonds. Highly esoteric.

In the chapter of her autobiography I was then perusing, *she* was the one in bonds, so to speak. I was reading how they took her into custody, locking her up behind the grimy walls of Holloway Prison soon after the war broke out ("I had no idea that dirt like that existed"). After the humiliation of being stripped and inspected for venereal disease, headlice and other unheard-of afflictions, she was assigned to a damp-walled cell twelve feet by seven with filthy mattress, grimy sheets and coarse blanket for furnishings—and with no charges having been laid. From some of the warders came the predictable verbal barbs exacerbated by envy and seasoned with power. Fortunately for her they themselves were under discipline.

My thoughts were all over the place, my wife Patricia was about to arrive from Germany for a few days and whatever that might mean I wanted to be part of it, I didn't have a copying stand and I didn't have flash, so I was flirting with failure by hand-holding my Olympus camera and photographing under lamps the books I chose to illustrate for the article I'd be sending off to Fredson Bowers, editor of *Studies in Bibliography*. I was using a macro lens, fast transparency film (400 ASA) and exposures of 1/250th of a second to obviate camera-shake, with correspondingly large aperture settings, all dicey. My luck held because they came out as sharp as could be expected in the circumstances and were printed together with the article in the 1992 volume.

I was getting through a chapter a day in the shop, reading that after several months her conditions improved until finally she and Mosley were accommodated together. After three years in prison they were released, no longer perceived to be a security threat. She hadn't been punished because of conviction of crime but for constituting a nebulous "public danger". That happens in wartime, and there were limits to my sympathy. They hadn't broken her spirit or changed her views in the slightest. Several years later she and her husband went to live in France in a house built for one of Napoleon's generals, called "*Le Temple de la Gloire*". They were in the Windsors' circle, which may have been depressing or interesting, probably the latter.

I generally follow my instincts, for better or worse. One day I was back down in the basement photocopying Lord Burlington's 1743 catalogue so that I could then make annotations on my own copy, when the Duchess's secretary (I think it was) happened to be there too, so I asked her was Lady Mosley still alive.

"Yes, she lives in France. She visits here from time to time."

I said I might write—did they have her address?

"Yes", and she wrote it down on a piece of paper and handed it to me.

I read it, carefully folded it and slipped it into the inside pocket of my jacket.

I did nothing for a long while after I'd returned home, then ultimately wrote off to her. I told her how I'd come by the address. I may have said I'd read her autobiography and that I'd like to ask her a few questions along lines she may have dealt with but not in detail. I probably suggested a few heads of inquiry, about her husband's philosophical outlook, for instance. Most people are flattered to be asked about their philosophical views—it's a rarefied line of inquiry, does honour to their intelligence, and in this case I thought it would be original, as I'd never read anything anywhere about the philosophical (as distinct from politico-philosophical) foundations of Mosley's thinking.

I would have mentioned other lines of inquiry that interested me. Nothing profound, certainly nothing soul-searching, merely the sort of questions that invite anecdotes, phrased in a courteous way. Diana Mosley was a highly intelligent, strong-willed person. To gain her confidence (and I wasn't being dishonest in this) I needed to show an understanding for her and her husband, and I did understand them after my fashion, in the contexts of the Great Depression and the turbulence of the times. I wasn't going to get anywhere if I wrote in a critical tone and I didn't, nowhere near critical. Of course from her account of her life in the late-1930s and her trips to visit Hitler in Berlin I understood perfectly well why she had been "secured", she had to be, but she could have been secured under house arrest with the phone lines tapped, and vastly more cheaply. The conditions as she described them would make the average reader sympathise with her.

She gave me the chance to do something for her, a personal favour, which I jumped at and in which I failed. It was a two-part mission. She asked me to read a book that had just been published on the subject of her incarceration, I did so, and the book certainly influenced me. As its imprint (one of my own publishers) shows, it was a serious study by A. W. Brian Simpson, *In the Highest Degree Odious: Detention without Trial in Wartime Britain* (Clarendon Press, Oxford, 1992). Lady Mosley's suggestion was that I might review it. I promised her I'd do so. I wrote a review and sent it off to *Quadrant*, then being edited by Robert Manne, but for whatever reason—perhaps a perceived lack of didactic intent, Robert being the didactic type—he didn't publish it. He may have thought I was defending the indefensible, which I wasn't. If Simpson's facts tended that way so be it.

Across a correspondence that ran several times in each direction I received some information in reply to my letters, not important information, mostly anecdotal because my questions invited anecdotes, and I have no comment to make on the answers.

I asked Diana Mosley to comment on the Depression and the general atmosphere in England, by way of contextualising everything else. She did so, and into the bargain compared the case of Germany. The underlinings are hers:

> I should have to write reams in order to answer it adequately. In the thirties England was so badly administered, what was called poverty in the midst of plenty, that millions of people were suffering from hunger, rotten slums to live in etc, and the politicians seemed quite unable to deal with the situation. England was by way of "owning" a quarter of the globe with unimaginable riches of every sort and yet this is how very many people lived. My husband came up with an answer which seemed and still seems valid. In fact I think it is admitted now that he was right. In Germany they also had poverty and suffering, 6 million unemployed. Hitler came and within 2 or 3 years the whole country was transformed. They had no external "riches" but Hitler said the real riches of a country were the people. As you know from what has happened since the mound of rubble Germany was in 1945, he was perfectly right. In the thirties there was quickly tremendous prosperity for all, new housing, splendid roads etc. It seemed a very rich and happy country, after having been a miserably poor one.

Then she added, "Hitler is to blame for the war, along with our own local war-lovers headed by Churchill. He is also to blame for appalling murders and horrors. Therefore everyone has forgotten his political genius, of before the war."

As I've indicated, I asked her about the philosophical influences on Sir Oswald Mosley, not just to flatter her but because I was genuinely interested to know. The answer was more than I'd expected and I've seen nothing to match it for concision and point in the biographies. I thought when I first read it that the detail and tone did the writer credit, and I wondered how many of my academic colleagues would even understand it:

> He was much influenced by Nietzsche. After he learnt German he could quote long passages by heart. He loved the poetry of it. He was influenced by Spengler (whom you may not consider a philosopher at all). He considered that the fact of science and its giant strides would enable the West to disprove Spengler's pessimistic conclusions. All in all, besides Plato, the philosophy that influenced his thinking most was Goethe's. He saw Nature as being the pattern for mankind to follow and he thought Goethe's theory of the stimulating influence of evil in the world profoundly interesting. He liked the idea of a *Pflanzschule* [the world as a nursery of souls] and never disbelieved in an after-life, saying we do not know and cannot know. He was not a Christian, I suppose he was a Pantheist.

There were other observations along similar lines but these were the most interesting.

I wrote in one of my letters that I'd noted that Magda Goebbels was a close friend of hers. What did she think of the action of Magda and Josef Goebbels in killing their children before they took their own lives? In her autobiography she'd almost appeared to justify it. What did *she* think they'd been thinking?—that the children might be raped or murdered by Russian soldiers? Or the fate of the children of the Czar and Czarina, shot with their parents in a basement room in Ekaterinberg by the Cheka? Then again, maybe they'd have been all right.

"I don't exactly defend Frau Goebbels's action", Diana Mosley confided to me, "I only say I understand it. Very possibly the Russians would have killed the children. Almost worse, they might have been scattered, and ill treated. The Allies (not sure which) were vile to Goering's wife and daughter." Then she went on to tell me "I was fond of Magda, a very loyal and sweet woman and loving mother."

I asked her what Hitler was like as company, understanding from what I'd read that she was sometimes alone with him in the Reich Chancellery in 1939.

"Hitler was a fascinator, as many people found. Part of the charm was his extreme naturalness and lack of affectation."

I asked her to comment on Hitler's view, as expressed to her, of Czechoslovakia and Munich, and I was writing that letter soon after Czechoslovakia had split into two states following the break-up of the Soviet Union and the end of the communist regimes in Eastern Europe, which explains how she answered.

"He thought Czechoslovakia a country manufactured at Versailles, bound sooner or later to split into its component parts. He did not think 'Munich' particularly important and thought England was using the whole 'crisis' as an excuse to attack Germany. His prophecy about the split of Czechoslovakia has now come true."

I asked her what other things they discussed during her visits to Berlin.

"I can't tell you much", she replied, "so long ago. We usually talked politics, the events of the day, or about politicians I knew. Once when I came from Paris he said how much he would love to go (he was by then too well-known for a private visit to be possible) and he said rather sadly, 'Cafés, Variétés, und ich gehe so gern ins Theater!' He loved seeing

Rome", she added, "and was excited by Michelangelo as architect, saying that he had told Speer to make cornices and mouldings deeper and more important since seeing the Capitol and St Peter's."

I asked her how he treated her.

"He was solicitous when I expected a baby, and very solicitous to Unity when she had pneumonia, sending his own doctor. Also of course when she shot herself." She said she was struck by the fact that "his manners were very ceremonious, but that is the German way."

I asked whether they ever watched films together or listened to music.

"Yes", she told me, "he would laugh and comment on films. I never listened to a gramophone with him", she added, "he liked conversation."

She went on to tell me that "He often spoke of England in a very complimentary way. I remember him saying England was fortunate to have 'diese kleine Prinzessin', Princess Elizabeth, then aged about 8. He asked once: 'Wie baut man jetzt in England?' and of course the answer was they built only villas and cheap housing. Of course he was the most interesting person on earth to talk to at that time, and so much depended upon him."

I asked her for her view of the 20 July 1944 bomb plot.

"I thought the bomb plot despicable. Stauffenberg, as a serving officer, had a pistol, he was in the bunker, he could have shot Hitler at close range. Instead, he planted a time bomb and ran away to Berlin hoping to head a new government. To shoot Hitler would have cost him his own life, but instead he chose to behave like the I.R.A. Hitler was not killed, but many of Stauffenberg's colleagues were, and many horribly maimed (for example General Bodenschatz, as I read after the war. I knew him slightly.)"

I suggested that had the plot succeeded, it would have shortened the war.

She disagreed. "I think the Allies would have gone on to the bitter end. Russia would have forced them to."

I asked her what she thought of the new regional nationalisms (in the former Yugoslavia, the Basque country, Catalonia, etc).

She told me her husband "always hoped that within Europe regionalism would flourish, and that for example it would solve the Irish problem." I thought it interesting that she chose to answer me with reference to what her husband thought—she was obviously still in love with him, but she was also thinking for herself. "Since the break-up of Yugoslavia", she added, "this may be over-optimistic. Unfortunately many people really love fighting."

I asked her view of the extreme right in Europe.

"Most parties of the extreme right", she told me, "are wedded to nationalism, which O.M. deplored as completely out of date." That Diana Mosley was wedded to the idea of the European Union didn't surprise me. Mosley had advocated what he called "Europe a Nation" in the 1960s. It's a concept with pre-war roots.

Lady Mosley told me as clearly as she could put it that "I still regard the war as a terrible crime against Europe and I blame him [Hitler] for setting it in motion", and then went on to say that she had no regrets about continuing to oppose the war after 3 September 1939: "We campaigned for peace during the 'phoney war'. I am thankful, despite the horrors of the [English] prisons, that we did so. None of the war atrocities could have happened in peace, and a civilized solution to minority problems was perfectly possible. It looks as if Europe *will* be made, despite English dragging of feet."

That was the early 1990s. Had she lived to see the degree to which the European Union's higher bureaucracy would assume ever-widening powers through the early decades of the twenty-first century, with the European parliament little more than a rubber stamp, one wonders whether she'd have been quite as enthusiastic, but there we are: the EU as the realisation of a Fascist goal (among other things, of course).

Because Diana Mosley was almost deaf (as she told me), these conversations had to be conducted by post. What made the exercise an experience for me was not so much the information at the end of it, largely original, interesting, though not terribly important. It was the path itself, the way I'd come across this woman at second-hand, flipping through the pages of a book with its photographs of her when she was young, in the house of her sister who was so friendly and helpful to me in the course of my work on Lord Burlington's library, wrapped up in the atmosphere of that place in an otherwise cold and empty spring.

7

Children of the Iranian Revolution

In late 1986 I was planning a trip to Paris to interview Valéry Giscard d'Estaing at his Paris house, but I wanted to avoid the conventional routes and to stop over along the way. Anywhere I was likely to come across more than three or four tourists was out. I could spend a week exploring remote Shinto shrines in Hokkaido. I could fly via Vladivostok, stop over at Novosibirsk and take a boat trip up the Ob. I could go by Colombo and put up at the wonderful old Galle Face Hotel. Certain stopovers ruled themselves out and one of those was Iran, then in the midst of a full-scale war imposed by Saddam Hussein (and parenthetically backed by the United States).

Iran was seven years down its revolutionary road, a path entirely new. British and American reporters were finding it particularly difficult to gain entry, and as far as I knew there were no Australian journalists working out of Tehran, though I've never checked that. Because a stopover in Iran seemed impossible it exercised my mind. Perhaps a carefully worded approach just might be successful. I wrote off to the

Canberra Embassy of the Islamic Republic of Iran requesting a visa, saying I wanted to spend a few days in Tehran *en route* to Paris, that I was open-minded, not predisposed against their revolution, and that on my return home I'd write an article for the papers about what I'd seen. A few days later I received a short response from some second-level official: "Application rejected."

My second letter went into an envelope addressed to the Ambassador, His Excellency Ahmad Attari, and underlined Personal and Confidential, saying the same thing but more warmly. I may even have said I sympathised with their attempt to reclaim the religious dimensions of their culture, which was at least partly true, and I may have wished God's blessings upon him, and would have meant it. Needless to say I didn't agree with some of the consequences, to do with individual rights, that go with the reclamation of traditional culture, but I left that unsaid.

It was two days later, around 4.00 p.m., I'd just pulled up outside my house and as I was opening the front door the telephone was ringing—I had one of those old black bakelite affairs sitting on its matching ringer base and it was very shrill, as if there was always an emergency. By contrast the voice on the other end was soft or there was something wrong with the line, because the conversation went like this:

"Hello?"

"Hello??"

"*Hello!!!*"

"Dr Ayres?"

"Speaking."

"This is Ambassador Attari, Embassy of the Islamic Republic of

Iran. I'm calling regarding your request for a visa to visit Iran."

"*Yes*, Excellency. Thank you, thank you for calling!"

"May I ask, when would you like to visit Iran exactly, please?"

I gave him the dates I had in mind.

"Very good, and… would you like it if I could arrange for someone to meet you at the airport?"

"That would be *most* kind, Excellency. I'd appreciate that very much."

"Very well then, I'll arrange for someone from the Department of Islamic Guidance to meet you. I'll need to know all the details, your flight number and so on. You can go ahead and make those airline bookings now. Then please send the details to me here, together with your passport, and I'll have it visaed and returned to you within a few days." Words to that effect.

So for the reasonable fee of $35 my passport was visaed and I left for Paris via Tehran. I assured him he wouldn't regret it, and he didn't.

"In the name of God the Merciful, the Compassionate, I welcome you aboard this Iran Air flight to Tehran." It was right on 10.15 a.m. in the Persian Gulf, 23 November 1986, and the words from the captain had a highly reassuring effect on me. I was seated towards the front of the plane, on the left, a window seat. Outside, the walkways were disengaging from the Boeing 747 SP and the engines were warming up. As the plane began its slow taxi to one of the runways the pilot came back on the intercom: "In compliance with the principles of the Islamic Republic of Iran we request that women continue to wear their scarves during the course of the flight. Thank you." The request may have been general or just intended for Westerners, not that there were many on this flight. I was curious about the young woman sitting beside me, nicely dressed. I assumed she was Persian and I debated whether I'd talk to her. Better not, I thought, but within minutes she opened a conversation.

The flight was uneventful. I had a soft drink, straight Coke, nothing harder on offer. Ninety minutes later we landed at Tehran's Mehrabad Airport. I'd never seen anything like it. It came home to me that it really was wartime here. Brown-and-beige C130 transport planes and fighter aircraft easily outnumbered airliners. The largest camouflage net I've ever seen was draped over a Boeing 747, entirely covering it. I counted three F4 Phantom fighter-bombers and two F14s parked along our taxiing route.

As we disembarked onto the tarmac and into a warm kerosene-fumed breeze an F4 tore across the sky directly above and landed a minute later, deploying its drag chute. The previous day, I learned, the Iranians had fired another surface-to-surface missile into Baghdad, so I assumed they were on high alert for any Iraqi retaliatory strike.

We were queued up waiting to pass through Customs, the lines stretched forever and I was towards the back. This was obviously going to take some considerable time. Suddenly, however, a young bearded guy walked past calling my name. When I identified myself he took me by both hands as if we were long-lost friends, introduced himself and said "Just come with me."

He was actually holding my hand as we walked, which I thought especially nice, and we went straight past the long queues and up to the desk where he showed his card and said a few words, perhaps half a dozen. We were waved straight past and there were no more formalities for me.

"I have a car outside" he told me.

It turned out to be an Iranian-assembled Hillman Hunter. They were everywhere in Tehran, together with plenty of BMWs and other European makes. We were out of the airport in a couple of minutes and already I was being made to feel at home.

"You're interested in the Revolution?" Mohammad asked after introducing me to his young friend at the wheel.

"Well, yes."

"That's good, because I want to make a program for you, but you're not here for long, so it will be rushed. Is there anything in particular that you'd like to see?"

"I want to get a feeling for how things have changed here", I told him, and I made a few suggestions. "You could show me a university, perhaps the Parliament, shops, markets, housing projects, and I'd like to see the symbolic fountain of blood at the war cemetery, that sort of thing. The former American Embassy, of course—have to see that, at least from the outside. I guess we wouldn't be able to do all of those. I'm happy to be guided by you."

He booked me into a hotel, the Intercontinental, and left me for a couple of hours so that I could take a shower and change, after which he returned and suggested a preliminary walk.

I don't wish to sound like those visitors to the Soviet Union under Stalin who reported on a workers' paradise, so I'll present a contrasting view later on, but I have to say I was surprised to find the streets as clean as they were and in such good repair, considering how many years' resources of the state had been directed to fighting an imposed war. Almost all the streets were treed, many of the trees planted recently under a scheme to ameliorate urban unemployment. Only once did I see someone begging. These things can't be staged.

Everywhere there were soldiers in uniform, on leave or about to go to the front, most of them volunteers. Up at the front, thousands were dying in every charge, in battles not unlike those on the Western Front in 1915–16 and equally fruitless, and the intake was getting younger by the month. The only alternative seemed to be a humiliating peace and the loss of territory. A local newspaper referred to "this nation of 27 million soldiers," a garrison state.

"What makes you think you're going to win this war?" I asked.

"There's no doubt about that, we'll win it. Maybe the West will engineer the overthrow of Saddam Hussein, knowing that it's our condition for peace, or our victories will bring him down."

He told me about an elite new corps of 100,000 troops just then heading for the front, made up in part of 10,000 former Iraqi prisoners who now wished to fight for ideological rather than nationalist reasons. My first reaction was scepticism, before it dawned on me that those men were probably Iraqi Shia from the south. I had no independent sources in regard to anything I saw or was told. Anything I would write about all this would be one-sided. The whole point of the excursion was to listen to *their* side, largely silenced in the West. Then I was told that other Iraqi prisoners (again, probably Shia) had just sent a letter, written with their blood and published in black in the *Tehran Times*, to President Ali Khamenei (not to be confused with the supreme religious leader Ayatollah Khomeini), requesting "to be sent to the battlefronts to fight the aggressor Baathist forces". It wouldn't have been fun being an Iraqi prisoner in Iran at that time. I don't think any Christian Iraqis would have been changing sides, for they were generally well treated under Saddam, whose foreign minister, Tariq Aziz, was a Christian.

My guide, whose first name was Mohammad, worked for the Ministry of Public Guidance. He was twenty-seven and held a bachelor degree in language and translation. As we walked through the streets it was clear how proud he was of what his revolution had achieved. On the other hand he seemed reluctant to be included in any of the photographs I was taking. I've often wondered why. Did he feel that his revolution was less than a hundred per cent secure? Did he feel there was a one per cent chance I was a spy of some description?

"Look at this street and all these people", he commented as we walked along. "Everything here, down to the contents of the shops, is Persian, made right here. Eight years ago you'd look around at the people and say 'Who's *she* supposed to be? Sophia Loren? And over there, who's *that* person pretending to be?'" It occurred to me that the women all dressed much alike now, though I didn't say it. No burqas, of course, not among Persians, or none that I saw.

My friend continued with his remembrance of things past. "If you want to colonise a country, first destroy its culture. That's the principle the Americans work to. Eight years ago our people's pride in their culture was very low. The shops were full of Western fashion magazines, pornography, all the worst features of Western culture—because we recognise also the many *good* aspects of that culture." For the record, I wrote most of this up at the time, so the direct speech is pretty right.

He led me into a small supermarket. "Let's just walk around here for a while. Look at all these products—almost all these canned foods are Iranian, and all these packaged products also. Under the Shah you would have seen a high percentage of imported products here. Imported meant good." We entered fish shops, butcher shops, and a bakery in which people were buying flat bread straight out of glowing, cavernous earth ovens in which it's baked to order. The country was in the throes of a terrible war and yet I saw no long queues of people waiting for food, and the shops were full of produce. You can't fake that. Autarchy actually seemed to work here in ways good for the country and its economy, limited ways of course. This was wartime but I saw far fewer signs of a war economy than I'd expected, although petrol was strictly rationed.

We went back out into the street and uphill to where Mohammad lived. "When I remember how things were, when I look around at all this now, these streets, the people, the shops, it all feels *clean*."

"What percentage of the people would oppose the revolution?" I asked, although I had a pretty good idea of the answer I'd receive.

"Very few. Many of the rich, of course, because as the Imam has said, this is a revolution of the poor against the rich. Also those in the middle class who were totally Westernised. This is a Persian revolution, not based on some imported nineteenth-century teaching, but a revolution that's restored to the people its *own* culture."

He explained how they had eliminated usury from their banking system, a development of which the government was very proud. Under arrangements in force from 1983, deposits in a bank made the depositor a shareholder, in effect. The funds were invested in development projects—it might be an orchard, for instance—and one received a dividend according to the success of the project. The World Bank at that stage was already interested in the idea, which later, in the twenty-first century, would be offered by major banks in numerous countries including in the West.

We'd reached his flat, close to the school where his wife taught French. It was comfortable and spacious. I removed my shoes and he apologised for the fact that there were no chairs—regarded by him and his wife as a Western intrusion. We sat instead on cushions scattered on the Persian carpets. There was a colour television with a photograph of the Imam, Ayatollah Khomeini, on top.

While I was having a cup of tea, eating pomegranates and sweet lemons and looking through a book of photographs dealing with the war, Mohammad was in a separate room doing his ablutions and proceeding to pray. Then at 4.15 p.m. his wife returned from work. I was stupid enough to offer to shake her hand. "It's against Islamic custom for you to shake hands with me," she explained, "but don't apologise". Her English was minimal but she spoke perfect French and questioned me about Australia. They don't like England very much in Iran, to put it mildly. I got that from both sides. Even the United States is better. France is OK and Germany too. I made sure to point out that I was on my way to France and not to England.

After a while she suggested we watch television as the news was about to start. The newscaster was a woman, as were a lot of the announcers on various programs. I was reminded by her that women were in the forefront of the revolution. I already knew that—the television coverage I'd seen at home of the massive demonstrations against the Shah back in 1979 proved it. And unlike in Saudi Arabia, at least most of the professions seemed to be open to women. In one or two professions, of course, Islam positively encourages women professionals. Fifty per cent of medical patients are daughters and wives, obviously, and many of them prefer their gynecologists to be women. There were women members of the Majlis or Parliament. Iran Air had no women pilots at the time, but do now. How many women in professions supported the regime in the 1980s was anyone's guess but I got the distinct impression from the women academics I met that many of them didn't.

The news was preceded by military music, and most of the items were war-related, but there was considerable attention given to the Reagan Administration's acute embarrassment over its arms shipments to Iran (the Iran–Contra Affair)—not only had Iran got the arms it long ago paid for, but the Great Satan was now suffering an attack of acute embarrassment as a consequence—a double blessing, evidently, or triple if the minor part played by the Little Satan was also taken into account.

"Would you like to meet some people in the Parliament?" my hostess asked me. I explained that I was only there for two more days. "That's a pity. We could introduce you to Rafsanjani. You should stay longer. You could even meet the Imam."

"Khomeini?"

"It's not so difficult," she replied, explaining that the leaders here were not removed from the people—especially young people like my hosts, it seemed. Probably true.

Her brother arrived. "Why not stay here instead of at the hotel," they asked. I politely declined. I also declined an invitation to share dinner that evening, explaining that I already had a dinner appointment with the ambassador of one of the embassies, but readily agreed to come for dinner the following evening.

The next day, after looking at slum development projects along the way, we arrived at the office of the University Crusade (*their* English translation, oddly enough, of "Djahad Daneshgahi" or academic jihad) at Tehran University. University Crusade was among the institutions that emerged from the Islamic Revolution. Founded in 1980 by the supreme authority on educational and university matters, the Council of the Cultural Revolution, its purpose was to revolutionise the universities. Its members included professors, researchers and students, and its activities at the time I was there extended beyond ideology and propaganda into the laboratories and research centres where its committees conducted work across a wide spectrum of disciplines.

Among its then-current scientific projects were research on amyl nitrite and the neutralisation of the effects of chemical bombs, design and manufacture of aircraft vision systems, the remote control of heavy vehicles, techniques for recognising chemical gas, the manufacture and production of optic systems for various weapons, and the production of solid fuels for rockets. In these respects it obviously contributed to military self-reliance. At the same time, other teams were at work on such projects as "the principles of Islamic physical education," "Orientalists in the service of colonisation" (a study of the mind-set of Western Orientalists, *à la* Edward Said's book *Orientalism*), and "colonial influence through morality and behaviour."

Not all of their activity was on research, however. Day-to-day politics were given high importance. Some members of the Crusade I met were painting red slogans on long, white cotton sheets destined to join the dozens of other banners draped throughout the university. Through this office I met the head of the Department of English Language and Literature, a man whose dedication to the revolution was clear not only in what he said but in smaller matters like his green military-style jacket, extremely popular at the time. A beard, or absence of beard, was politically significant. He wore a beard. No one I saw wore ties, another factor of politico-cultural significance. The professor informed me that he was about to conduct a departmental meeting, scheduled for 11 a.m. Would I like to accompany him and meet his colleagues?

We entered the staff room where about 25 members of staff were seated about, women and men in roughly equal numbers but grouped separately. The professor introduced me and invited me to address his colleagues, which I did for ten or fifteen minutes, telling them about my own university, the nature of our literature classes, courses, assessment procedures, research activities.

I asked whether I could put some questions to them. How had the teaching of English literature changed here as a result of the political processes of the past seven years?

"As far as my own teaching of literature is concerned", replied one man without a beard and about 40 years of age, "not at all." "Mine neither," replied another. "For me, the question is very technical," a woman lecturer offered, "and would require a long and complex answer." That interested me.

I asked about the content of their courses. A woman lecturer told me that in her view a major study of English literature should have chronological coherency and cover a wide range of periods, a view consistent with my own. I pointed out that at home this concept was a thing of the past, that our students could pretty well choose what periods and courses they liked, with just a couple of period constraints. "If you like the arrangement you've just outlined," I assured her, "you wouldn't like our current arrangement at all. You'd despise it."

Someone suggested an academic exchange between our two universities. Where was I going from Tehran, another asked. "Paris, and after a few days there, from Paris direct to Atlanta," I replied.

"For most of us here," a woman of about thirty told me, "going to Paris is just a dream. Most of us would love to travel to France and other Western countries."

"Why?" asked my friend Mohammad, who had accompanied us to the meeting.

"*Why???* To experience other societies and meet other people, of course", another woman told him with a laugh. "Isn't it *obvious*?" Everyone was smiling at him, and not in sympathy. Evidently realising he'd made himself look silly in their eyes, he indicated it was time to go, so I thanked the department for welcoming me. "From what you've told me about your course structures and content", I told them, "the study of English literature is in better hands at the University of Tehran than in some places I could name."

Back in the Crusade office we had a very basic rice-based student meal, a dish suited to wartime. I asked one of the students whether there was still any armed resistance to the revolution, having read some weeks earlier of a deadly bomb blast in Tehran. He looked puzzled.

"He means the Marxist Mujahideen," another explained. They all smiled. "We finished it with them in 1983. The bomb was planted by Iraqi agents." I said I thought the Marxist Mujahideen had *become* Iraqi agents, and they liked that.

It was early afternoon and we were at the Museum of Reversion and Admonition, the new name for the Sa'd-abad Palaces where the Shah had his summer palace, along with other palaces including that of the Queen Mother.

"No wealth is amassed unless a poor man is deprived of bread and no palace is erected unless a shack lies beside it," Imam Ali observed long ago, and for all the trickle-down and the inflating cake, who can deny it if he's ever visited Bombay, Manila or Detroit? Anyway, it was a common theme at this museum.

"Go through the Earth, and behold what has been" was another motto in the booklet someone handed me, which put the palaces in their place: they are history. Among the documents left behind by the former residents and on display is one of the Royal Physician's daily reports on the Shah's mother:

> Her Royal Highness was feeling well and had no particular complaints. She did not cough at all today. She defecated twice, quite normally. Her vital data were normal. She was in a quite happy mood. At 9.30 a.m. she drank a glass of grape juice, and for her lunch she had a sufficient quantity of soup and "bagalapolo," complete with a dessert

> of bananas. From 2.15 p.m. to 4.40 p.m., she took a serene nap. Today, the resting position of Her Royal Highness, which is usually to the right, was changed to the left, which had a most beneficent effect on her health. In the evening, she had some honey milk-shake, and walked six times. At 7 p.m. she went to the lower floor reception hall, and at 10 p.m., returned to her bedroom. She was feeling very well and had no complaints. She slept from 10.50 p.m. to 7.30 a.m.
>
> For breakfast, she had a honey milk-shake, and then walked six times the length of the corridor.

I couldn't really see much wrong with all that. It certainly made me want a honey milkshake. We were standing outside this "Palace of the Tyrant's Mother" when, at 2.04 p.m., the air raid sirens sounded all across the city, not that anyone took the least notice—135 kilometres southwest of the capital the air space of the holy city of Qom had just been violated by an Iraqi warplane, which automatically set off the red-alert sirens in Tehran. The following day several western Iranian cities were hit, resulting in scores of civilian casualties.

For the rest of the day we strolled through markets and mosques and visited an Armenian Orthodox church, one of several. Mohammad told me there had been a considerable number of "martyrs" from among its flock. "Do you mean to say," I asked him, "that Christians who die in this war are also regarded as martyrs?" "Most definitely," he assured me.

I don't think he was right, indeed I was assured a year later by fighters in Afghanistan (who were Sunni, however, not Shia) that he was wrong. However, from what I can gather, both major streams of Islam teach that the Christian who fights for a Muslim country should be thanked, and as for the hereafter, though all the authorities may say he shall go to Hell, the final word is always that "Allah knows best," which surely leaves open the possibility of grace, though one would need to check on that.

Back in the car, we drove past the "Den of Spies," the former American Embassy, its walls completely painted over with slogans. Other walls were decorated with caricatures of Saddam Hussein in various states of terror or embarrassment. I made some reference to patriotism. "It's a patriotic war, yes" I was told, "but first it's an ideological war." Of course most of the people I was mixing with were ideological types.

I was at the centre of an Islamic renaissance besieged by its enemies, but what surprised me was the almost fraternal attitude to Christians I found among some of the revolution's young militants. I'm not referring to converts who have been turned from Islam, who are harshly regarded and often treated badly, especially if they then try to proselytise. The Orthodox and Catholics seemed respected among those I met, but to what extent that was manufactured for my benefit I can't say. They didn't treat me as someone bound for Hell. From what I understand, their scholars never ascribe their sometimes-harsh teachings, even those in the Koran, directly to God, but only indirectly to God through his admittedly imperfect Messenger, his recorder, which is close to but not quite the same thing. The relation of the Prophet Mohammad to God is not one of union as with Jesus (whom they revere as one of God's Messengers and of virgin birth, whose death was merely apparent and who will return in glory and as judge). Whatever the texts may say, the final decision is deferred to God, defined by his compassion and mercy.

In the evening we shared dinner at the flat, a family affair. I was leaving the following day. "If you can manage to return early in the New Year", Mohammad assured me, "I can arrange for you to visit the war front, but you will need to get in touch early so things can be arranged and co-ordinated." The television was showing fighters heading for the front deep inside Iraq. A ceremonial march-past in Prussian tradition followed. I said I'd think about it, and instantly forgot about it.

I wandered the aisles on the non-stop Iran Air flight to Paris and struck up a conversation with an Iranian businessman sitting at some distance from me, and then moved to sit with him. I told him what I'd seen and been shown. He was particularly amiable, offering a view of the revolution diametrically opposed to that of the young people who had hosted me.

He asked me straight-out "How many people in this plane do you suppose support the Government?"

"I wouldn't have any idea. They're obviously affluent people, very well dressed, better dressed than you'd see on any plane in Australia, businessmen, married couples—I'd say they're all middle class or significantly higher, so… twenty per cent?"

"Lower."

"*Ten* per cent?"

"*Zero* per cent, Philip—although that young bearded man back there, I have my doubts about him."

In his view hardly anyone in the whole of Iran supported the Government, which was composed largely of hypocrites.

He seriously proposed the theory, mentioned to me by my embassy friend as favoured by many in the upper and middle classes, that Khomeini was an agent of the British. The theory goes that the Americans replaced the disliked British, so the disliked people who have thrown the Americans out must be agents of the British. This theory had some currency. In order to account for a revolution with which they could not identify, some Westernised Iranians had turned to fantasy. Or maybe there's something in it.

There was one achievement of the revolution of which my flight companion approved. "They have destroyed Marxism in Iran totally and literally. No Shah could have achieved that." There were some left, he said, but they were now located on the Iraqi side of the border, and under Saddam Hussein's protection.

Far to the south the eight-year war continued—two more years to go and hundreds of thousands of additional dead to go with it. From this height it was an abstraction.

"Look down there, to the right," he told me. "—Mount Ararat."

As we descended towards Charles de Gaulle Airport he drew my attention to the stewardesses seated nearby.

"Watch them. That one's applying nail polish, see? And her friend: lipstick on already, and now lip gloss. Nothing to stop them, huh? When we get out, the first place they'll go will be the women's lavatories. They'll rip that stuff off and switch into their Western clothes. I fly regularly and it happens every flight."

For years afterwards Ambassador Attari would send me Christmas cards, some of them with short poems of his, inscribed. He liked the article I published. After Attari returned to Iran the Embassy continued to send copies of the English-language airmail edition of the *Tehran Times* each week. I've always intended to return. Their fruits are the best I've tasted, and from Tehran it's a short drive to the mountains that overlook the city replete with their magnificent high-altitude ski runs. It's over thirty years on and some of my friends have been there recently. They loved the place and the people they met.

Gulbuddin Hekmatyar with the author, Peshawar, November 1987. But which was the real Empire of Evil? Author photo.

8

Jihadists in Afghanistan

In early 1987 I received a telephone call from Senator Richard Alston, then one year into his parliamentary career. He'd read the article I'd published in the Saturday *Age* on my trip to Iran and wondered whether I might be interested in joining him as an Australian-born member of the newly-formed Afghan-Australia Council, of which he was President. The other non-Afghan on the Council was the Anglican Archbishop of Melbourne, David Penman. The membership included Afghans with connections to the leadership of the various jihadist groups warring against the Soviet-backed government of Afghanistan.

There were seven Afghan political parties centred in the Pakistani frontier city of Peshawar, and the party with which I was put in contact and travelled was Hezb-i-Islami—the Islamic Party of Afghanistan. I chose this party not out of any particular political sympathy but because the person with whom I had become most friendly on the Council, Sher Keshtiar, had contacts with them at a senior level, and because I'd heard that they were strong, well-heeled and well-equipped. It was the most ill-considered thing I'd done up to that point. Sher asked if I'd write a major article like the Iran article for the same newspaper based on an itinerary he said he would organise through his connections in Islamabad and Peshawar. I said that, if I agreed, I would travel on my own account. Once we'd begun discussing the project I effectively became locked-in. If in two minds, don't flirt.

In preparation for the trip I read U.S. State Department reports on Afghanistan, courtesy of Richard and the Parliamentary Library in Canberra, and invested in warm clothing, camera lenses covering the range from 28 to 300 mm, and ten rolls of fine-grain 50 and 100 ASA Kodachrome. I also carried a Sony Walkman Professional tape recorder and several blank tapes. From my reading I learned or deduced that Hezb-i-Islami seemed to be the favourites of the Pakistani Government under General Zia-ul-Haq, and the favourites too of Pakistan's Inter-Services Intelligence (ISI), and most of their funding came from the United States Government via the Central Intelligence Agency on the understanding they would use most of that money to buy first-class military equipment from China *via* intermediaries and/or the black market.

I was later understandably criticised by some of my Melbourne Afghan friends for giving Hezb-i-Islami publicity. Certainly they were the most extreme of the Afghan resistance forces and would later develop close field relations with the Taliban and al Qaeda following the United States' invasion of Afghanistan in 2002. At least one of the friendly acquaintances I made in Peshawar ended up imprisoned and tortured by the Americans at Bagram, and it was said that one or two others were at Guantanamo Bay. But whatever group I had gone with, it would have been the wrong group in the eyes of some Melbourne Afghans. I liked them all and wished to displease none. The reason their community leaders had asked Senator Alston to preside over their

Council was precisely because they were politically divided—he acted as a vital unifying factor, as well as a voice for their cause in Parliament. I watched his impressive leadership of these people at close quarters over several years. They needed someone of status and above all of diplomatic ability (years later Richard was appointed Australian High Commissioner to the United Kingdom).

Before going, I already knew something about the leader of Hezb-i-Islami, whom I'd meet soon enough. This was Gulbuddin Hekmatyar. He'd studied engineering at Kabul University in the early 1970s, and during his university years had been an activist within the People's Democratic Party of Afghanistan (PDPA), the Moscow-line communist party. I didn't know at that stage that he'd been jailed for allegedly ordering the killing of a Maoist student, or that in his subsequent Islamist incarnation he was said to have thrown acid into the face of a female student for not wearing a veil. Having undergone a 180-degree ideological change, following his release from jail he joined the Organization of Muslim Youth. Later the Organization split and Hekmatyar founded the radical Hezb-i-Islami, pseudo-Leninist in organization but anti-Marxist in philosophy. They believed in taking power through armed struggle, in contradistinction to Professor Burhanuddin Rabbani's more moderate but also Islamist Jamiat-e-Islami. The distinctions were complex and whatever one says about them is simplification.

I landed in Islamabad just before midnight on 30 November 1987 and was met at the airport by three young men in brown woollen Afghan caps and green army jackets. My first impression was that they were comfortably off, reinforced minutes later by their late-model Land Cruiser in which we drove through block after block of the capital's straight, deserted streets to a guarded safe house in one of the leafiest and most pleasant districts of the city. It was late, and after talking awhile we turned in.

The most senior of these young men was Dr Ghairat Baheer, Gulbuddin Hekmatyar's son-in-law, a highly educated, tall and self-possessed young man with a lot of charm. His father-in-law knew what he was doing when he made him his chief spokesman. After 2002 he would spend six years as a political prisoner of the Americans at their detention facility close by Bagram Air Base in Afghanistan, incessantly bombarded with extremely loud, Satanic-sounding rock music to break his spirit. To be imprisoned by a foreign power in one's own country must count as a kind of honour, and I assume that his calm demeanour emanated from interior qualities that enabled him to emerge with his sanity intact. Following his release in 2008 he headed-up negotiations with the Karzai Government and the Americans, who evidently respected him.

The next morning we did the three-hour drive to Peshawar. The young man at the wheel, Mahmoud, was a product of Kabul's overcrowded political prison and its torture cells, where he'd spent a few years and emerged committed but psychologically skewed. "I'm not normal", he told me as we consumed mandarins and tossed the peel out the windows. Over the next few weeks I met others like him. The brother of the interpreter who later accompanied me into Afghanistan emerged from that prison deranged.

Peshawar is chaotic, noisy and dusty, the air is thick with carbon monoxide, and when I was there the random firing of assault rifles punctuated the nights. I was given an upstairs room in the Hezb-i-Islami guest house, regularly used as a meeting place by the leadership and guarded around the clock against attack from the Khad, the Afghan secret police whose *agents-provocateurs* frequently plant their bombs in the most crowded streets—one went off causing loss of life around the time I arrived.

In the guest house you ate and slept on the floor and were thankful for the unvaried rounds of flat bread, beef or mutton soup and green tea, knowing you were their special guest and not permitted to contribute to their running expenses. The visiting journalists generally stayed nearer to the centre of town, at Dean's Hotel or the Pearl Continental. Few of them wished to enter Afghanistan, though some did. West German parliamentarians had gone in across the border, and as part of my preparation I had written to Jean François Deniau, a deputy in the French National Assembly, who had published an article in *Encounter* magazine about his time with fighters in Afghanistan.

No Australian politicians had gone inside. I was informed that one foreign journalist had waited in Dean's Hotel over two months for the mujahideen to arrange a trip inside, finally growing tired of waiting and flying back to Europe. I was more fortunate. Staying in the guest house, I was able to talk at length to the political leaders of the party and treat the place (including the telephone) as my own. I visited their new military headquarters in the countryside, some of the worst refugee camps, and their hospitals. The Reagan–Gorbachev summit was imminent, so I was able to observe the rising anxiety and distrust with which it was viewed by the party's leadership.

Nawab Saleem was Hekmatyar's closest associate in Peshawar and I got to know him well. He handled their public relations and I understood he was Hekmatyar's biographer. I remember thinking that in any Hekmatyar-led government (and there would be one in 1996) he would probably head the Ministry for Information. Whether he did or not I have no idea. I talked with him on a number of occasions. He was a graduate of the University of Virginia and had an acute mind, was highly articulate and ideologically committed. Nawab was regularly at the guest house, we got on well and I made close notes of some of our conversations.

“People confuse us with Khomeini and the system in Iran, deliberately so as to discredit us”, he told me. “To us, Islam provides a complete and sufficient basis for a state, and the future Afghanistan will be a non-aligned Islamic republic, but we’re critical of Iran—hostage-taking, for example, is against Islam.” He thought the Iranians were bent on the expansion of Shia Islam (most Afghans are Sunni). “So we have closed our office in Teheran”, he told me.

I asked him whether he considered the Soviet Union the principal threat. “It’s currently the military enemy” he replied, “and it’s also the immediate cultural enemy within the country, but I would say the United States is the more dangerous cultural enemy.”

“You take their money.”

Yes, he went on, but that didn’t blind anyone to what they represented, which was an immensely powerful pervasive influence through the various media they dominated—a materialistic and superficially attractive, atomistic and synthetic culture divorced from its own Christian traditions, entertaining at best and pornographic at worst. That was the sum of what he was saying, adding that because it was so seductive, for a culture like his it was destructive. Any retaliation against it by Islamists would be defensive.

I said I thought American popular culture was a lot better than ancient Babylon’s, or Sodom’s (which he probably had in mind), that religion was still strong, as he must know having lived there, that America’s was a culture of contrasts and you couldn’t stereotype it. He agreed but said that he was referring to cultural reach, to Hollywood and the like, and that he could see the good side.

I first met Nawab in his office at their extensive military headquarters, built within a large defensive perimeter and with its central buildings surrounding a square courtyard. Over a thousand fighters, it was said, were or had been engaged in exercises there, and thousands of refugees lived in the surrounding district. I visited the political office and talked with other members of the leadership, almost all under forty years of age and most of them university-educated.

They were full of anticipation regarding the forthcoming Gorbachev–Reagan summit in Washington. Would the two leaders do a deal to restrict the role of the mujahideen in a future Afghan government? Would Reagan cut the supply of money in response to a Soviet withdrawal over a long timetable? (In the event, all Soviet forces would be withdrawn by early 1989, and the Soviet Union would begin to disintegrate soon afterwards). Some thought it wouldn't matter—they had enough munitions inside Afghanistan to fight for more than a year without resupply and most of Hezb-i-Islami's weaponry did not come from the United States but through the black market. Also, there was funding from Saudi Arabia. If they could wear down one superpower militarily, how could political pressure much affect them? Some form of interim coalition government might be strung together for a while by the superpowers, but subsequent elections would produce victory for the Islamist parties, they believed.

I was told about raids within the Soviet Union itself, news which the European press had reported but which I had not read in Australia, unsurprisingly given the paucity of column-inches devoted to international news in the Australian mainstream press. On several occasions majahideen had crossed the Oxus River and entered Soviet Tadzhikistan, hitting border posts in operations around the town of Moscovskiy, it was claimed. The borders were porous. They also boasted of having distributed cultural and religious literature inside Soviet Turkmeniya, Uzbekistan and Tadzhikistan, and 20,000 cassette recordings produced by the combined majahideens' Voice of Afghanistan. Some people in Soviet Central Asia, I was told, carried Hezb-i-Islami membership cards. Quite a few former Soviet Muslim soldiers were fighting with the mujahideen in northern Afghanistan. Ironically, they pointed out, the Soviet invasion of Afghanistan had increased Islamic activism inside the Soviet Central Asian republics (they cited the recent riots in Alma Ata) because of the example of successful resistance in Afghanistan, and they were also aware of rising nationalist sentiment in some of the more western republics like Chechnya, and in western China.

I spent a couple of days in the refugee camps of Akora Khattak and Munda. At that time there were more than three million Afghan refugees in Pakistan and another million in Iran, but of all the camps around Peshawar, Munda was the worst. Thousands of the recently arrived were unregistered and living in tents, the rest—scores of thousands—in mud houses that stretched for kilometres along narrow dirt streets with their makeshift shops and occasional school. There were five basic health units and though they were inadequate for the population I was surprised at how much could be done with such limited resources: each doctor was seeing up to 150 patients a day, vaccinating infants, controlling outbreaks of malaria, tuberculosis, diarrhoea and worm infestation, and providing once-weekly ante-natal and post-natal care. It's hard to convey how basic the facilities were.

I also visited a surgical hospital operated by Hezb-i-Islami in Peshawar where I photographed the meagre facilities and the patients, all of them war casualties. Thousands of patients passed through the wards each year and I was introduced to some of them—a child who had lost the bottom part of his leg to an anti-personnel mine, a man who had lost an entire leg, another with the back of his head blasted away, a man attached to a drip, the effectiveness of which he patiently awaited as he coughed blood into a bucket, another ceaselessly dabbing cotton balls onto a head wound and dropping them into a bucket half full of them. The smell was overpowering though the worst of it was submerged beneath the heavy scent of antiseptic. Ten doctors, trained at Kabul and Nangahar, were at work. I photographed the operating theatre. "It's not antiseptic, you can go in. We'll make it antiseptic before we operate", a doctor informed me.

By now Hekmatyar, a frequent visitor at the guest house together with one or two Saudis who I was told were important, was sick of waiting for the outcome in Washington and decided to stage a massive rally to denounce any Reagan–Gorbachev deal in advance—a Hezb-i-Islami initiative, not undertaken in concert with the other Peshawar parties that made up the "alliance". He confided in me his annoyances (I interviewed him at some length). One of his special hates was the word "fundamentalist".

"They take this word", he told me, "which is applicable to certain Protestant Christians, and apply it to Islam where it makes no sense. We believe in the political sufficiency of Islam, but 'fundamentalist' is meaningless. It shows you how stupid they are who talk like that." What I presumed he meant was that in Christianity the term "fundamentalist" distinguishes those who read the sacred text literally as opposed to those, including Catholics and many Protestants, who are prepared to read a lot of the Bible as truth-conveying allegory or myth. In Islam every word of the Koran is given its full literal value by every Muslim, and the arguments are about context and application, not allegory or myth. In that sense at least, Islam is necessarily "fundamentalist", and it's not a dividing issue among Muslims. But then ignorance is so deep in the West that President George W. Bush would later proclaim that he was on a "crusade" against al Qaeda.

The rally next day lasted three hours and was carefully programmed. Well-dressed children, somewhat like uniformed Boy Scouts or the USSR's Young Pioneers, sang mujahideen songs and made short speeches, there were addresses by mullahs, and a dozen or so young guards in green uniforms sang the songs of the struggle, all climaxing in the entry of Hekmatyar himself.

Whereas in an interview situation I thought he radiated tranquillity and spoke with deliberation, in front of a crowd one had a different impression. His voice was no longer subdued but took on a strident edge. He based his address, later printed in translation, on a verse from the Koran: "Mighty indeed were the plots which they made, but their plots were well within the sight of God, even though they were such as to shake the hills." Then he got into his stride. The Soviets wanted "to reach an accommodation over the Afghanistan of martyrs with Washington for the formation of an un-Islamic government acceptable to both, and thus to prevent the establishment of a purely Islamic government at the hands of our mujahideen. They are striving for the imposition of those decrepits and non-persons who had already been tested." But "the diabolical conspiracy" would fail. Then he outlined his party's demands: unconditional and immediate withdrawal of all Soviet forces and no communist participation in a future government. In a clear reference to the United States he said that the mujahideen "will consider any alien force under any name an aggression on our soil and resist it with all our might and force." In his windup to a fairly long speech he predicted "the definitive victory of our Islamic jihad" while stressing "the continuation of armed struggle as the only and decisive factor in the expulsion of foreign forces".

Meanwhile my trip into Afghanistan had taken shape. We left early the following morning and travelled down through the Tribal Areas to a border town and from there through nearby valleys into Afghanistan's Paktia Province.

The most impressive event I witnessed during my few days there was an evening rocket attack on the airstrips of the provincial capital of Khost. I was with a small group, including the commander, who advanced during the late afternoon to the top of a hill with commanding views over the air base below and the city four or five miles away. The mountains all around were invested ("infested" if you were on the other side) by Islamist forces opposed to the Soviet-backed government in Kabul which controlled most of the nation's cities and towns, though not much else, just like the situation the American-backed Government faces thirty years later. The air was cold but the snow in this region was still a month away. Before sunset I photographed the airstrip and the town through my 300-mm lens (five frames that, placed end-on-end, cover the entire strip), advised by my companions to keep my head low, as there was a government-controlled foothill just a kilometre away. You can see the men stationed there in the photographs I took—they're walking about unaware of us. Earlier I'd photographed the rest of our group in a valley two kilometres behind us, setting up their 122-millimetre rocket-launcher with the projectiles lying all about. I'd also photographed, at the insistence of my friends, a dead Soviet officer back on the steep slopes of this very hill. He looked to be a couple months out of it, and I found myself thinking, while I levered the film-advance repeatedly from different angles, how much more I had in common with him than with my companions, hospitable though they certainly were. Here were the mortal remains of a European sent to back up a secularist government that he believed, or his government believed, was on the side of progress. Someone at home was mourning him unaware that he lay unburied, an infidel and intruder. It reminded me of Aeneas and his lost and unburied friend Palinurus. As an infidel I qualified to bury him myself, but it was a foreign country and besides the ground was hard.

After sunset the defensive forces within the perimeters of the airfield began engaging in their regular night-time duel with an invisible enemy to be kept at bay at all costs, their shooting guided by red tracer bullets mixed in with the solids. The distances involved were two or three kilometres, which meant that the arcing tracers could be seen well before they passed by, unless perhaps they were coming directly at you. The defenders of the airfield had set up swivelling spotlights to illuminate the hillsides nearest the base, as if to say "We'll see you if you come". The town was dark but the main airstrip and control tower were lit up, red lights flashing in sequences of three.

The commander was speaking in Dari into his field radio to those in the valley behind, finally issuing the order to fire with the words "Allahu Akhba!" We heard the blast of the launch followed by the roar as the missile passed over us, and seconds later saw the white flash of its impact towards the end of the long runway. A transport plane abruptly took off. Another, about to land, was kept flying around and around while the party behind in the valley, guided in their aim by the commander beside me, fired off the rest of the rockets at intervals of five minutes or so.

The purpose of the exercise, which was undertaken regularly from varying positions, was to disrupt the night-time in-flight of supplies and provisions. Khost was besieged on all sides. The road from Kabul and Gardez was impassable to the government forces, though while I was there they were trying to re-open it, employing over 15,000 men and columns of tanks to do so. Khost was a microcosm of the entire war—a superpower, its command of the skies a thing of the past thanks to American shoulder-fired ground-to-air missiles (though high-altitude bombing continued), struggling to supply proxies holed up in a few provincial cities encircled by rebels armed to the teeth and fervent in faith.

With rockets falling one after the other about the runway, the other side responded in kind, but nobody seemed concerned. The missiles coming up from the air base passed high above and exploded uselessly against the mountainsides kilometres behind us. When most of the rockets the group had brought along had been fired the commander decided to return to safer areas. There was still no moon and we followed him in starlight, half-sliding and half-stumbling down the hill and back to the launcher. After tea with the men there we set off in the jeep, navigating the creek beds and hillsides totally unconcerned, because these hills, like ninety per cent of Afghanistan, were effectively free-go. The mountains were full of insurgent camps and their deep brick-lined tunnels were packed with munitions.

I saw and photographed hundreds of rockets—BM12s and the 122-millimetre variety—and hundreds of rocket-propelled grenades meant for use against armoured personnel carriers but also effective against low-flying helicopters, as well as immense numbers of heavy and medium automatic weapons. Every shepherd boy leading a donkey or camel carried his own Kalashnikov. During my stay inside I visited and photographed a number of mountain-top anti-aircraft gun emplacements, having tea with the men who manned and maintained them. I photographed a downed Soviet helicopter and talked to a group of captured government troops who were making a road for the mujahideen—they'd been taken prisoner a few weeks earlier and seemed in good spirits. Before leaving I had a last talk with Hezb-i-Islami's commander for the Khost region, Faiz Mohammad Khan. We'd slept inside his command headquarters, known as Jihad Wahl, within a central cave more than ten metres deep that accommodated up to fifteen of us beneath its steel-girdered, brick-lined ceiling. There was total security against anything short of a direct bomb hit, with a field telephone and even fluorescent lighting, and regular meals of beef broth (or it might have been lamb or goat), flat bread and tea. Years later al Qaeda had one of its training camps there or nearby.

Back in Peshawar I visited a French compound near the Hezb-i-Islami safe house and fell into conversation with a gentleman who warned me that someone co-ordinating medical supplies within Afghanistan had been killed by members of "your group", but it was hearsay and he gave no details. Moreover it made no sense. Either what he was retailing was a myth he'd picked up somewhere, or the person involved brought it on themselves, I thought. He mentioned other cases and said Hezb-i-Islami sometimes turned their guns on rivals including Professor Rabbani's more moderate Jamiat-e-Islami whose military commander was Ahmad Shah Massoud. I'd heard it asserted that apart from the region around Khost, Hezb-i-Islami were not particularly active on the ground in Afghanistan and rarely engaged in pitched battles, but in the next breath they'd be telling you how they turned their guns on rivals, so by those very accounts they had plenty of force on the ground, as well as confidence. Besides, everyone knew that certain local commanders had local agendas, so rightly or wrongly I discounted what I heard. In any case it was too late for warnings or regrets. All political parties lie about all their rivals all the time.

Almost fourteen years later, on the evening of Tuesday 11 September 2001, I had dinner at the Sydney home of close friends John and Nancy Stone and was driven back to the Australian Club by John around 10.00 p.m. Up in my room, overlooking Macquarie Street and Sydney's Botanical Gardens, I mixed a Bloody Mary from ingredients in the minibar and switched on a U.S.-based cable channel. They were interrupting their program to go to New York, where it seemed an aircraft had crashed into one of the twin towers at the World Trade Center. There wasn't much smoke yet, and the announcers were unsure of what had happened. I watched the events unfold until about 2.30 a.m., by which time the entire bottom half of Manhattan was covered with clouds of smoke and dust and the towers were rubble. The President subsequently said it had been done by those "who hate our freedom", and that there'd be a crusade against them. Geoffrey and Ann Blainey were staying there too and in the morning we breakfasted together. "We're going to have to hear about this over and over, for months now", Geoffrey commented. "We'll be in for a long run of replays and a selective variety of analyses."

Malcolm Fraser with General Aidid, Mogadishu, 1992. "CARE thought it was safe in Bardera because it was your town, General, but our confidence was misplaced." Author photo.

9

The Road to General Aidid

He was courteous to those I was with and there was nothing instinctively to *dis*like about General Mohamad Farrah Aidid. The evil character who goes under his name in the film *Blackhawk Down* is a figment of Hollywood's imagination, though the film gets this much right: Aidid knew how to hit back. His regular political vocabulary, which I regret to say he spared us, was the Somali version of scientific Marxism–Leninism and a pleasure to quote, as I'll do.

It was at Una Fraser's ninetieth birthday reception at Melbourne's Alexandra Club in mid-1992 that her son Malcolm, then President of CARE International, suggested, "if you're interested", that I might travel to Somalia a week or two ahead of his team to see at first hand CARE's work in the famine-afflicted country. How I got there was my own affair he told me, but he thought that at Mombasa I should be able to find an aid-agency plane to fly me into Mogadishu, where I could stay at the CARE compound, observe their work in the city, and travel in one of their vehicles to the centre of the famine at Baidoa where his daughter Phoebe was in charge of the aid work. When he and his team arrived in Somalia, he said, I could fly around with them, and then later, back home, I could write about the work CARE was doing there, much as I'd written about his work with the Commonwealth Eminent Persons Group in South Africa.

Subsequently he gave me satellite-linked telephone numbers for CARE Mogadishu (run by Major Rhodri Wynn-Pope, formerly of the Grenadier Guards, later married to Phoebe Fraser). He said I could call them from the airbase at Mombasa to let them know when I'd be taking off and by which plane, in order to be picked up by a secure vehicle on landing. It was all entirely *ad hoc.* I made my own arrangements and had no idea what I was getting myself into, nor a great deal of interest, certainly not any particular interest in famines and their alleviation, but a degree of curiosity. He knew that if he suggested it over a couple of drinks I wouldn't be averse.

So after departing for Zimbabwe on 1 October I reached Harare the same day, stayed overnight at Meikles Hotel and flew next morning to Nairobi and on to Mombasa, where at Nyali Beach I found a very pleasant resort indeed.

Some of the aid agencies put their people up at Nyali Beach for their days off, as I discovered. It's one of those delightful hotels from which second-rate journalists on assignment in East Africa and the Middle East file their first-hand reports. Butchery in Rwanda?—"Reporting from Kenya". Civil war in Beirut?—"Reporting from Tel Aviv". They may as well be filing from London or New York. There are of course numerous and courageous exceptions like the late and admirable Liz Jackson whom I met while travelling along a remote road in Somalia. Certainly nothing happens at Nyali Beach, but it does offer gorgeous grounds in which I spent a day and a half killing time over pina coladas between visits to the military air base adjacent to Mombasa airport, where I managed to secure a free flight into Mogadishu on a Luftwaffe C160 Transall ferrying food aid. I spent the two-hour trip, mostly over water, in the back of the plane with the supplies, discovering that the stand-up lavatory was a pull-out chute in the left side of the fuselage.

The article I wrote on my return was largely about CARE's work in Somalia, but I was more interested in the politics behind the famine, the focus here. Somalia illustrated the consequences to traditional societies of imported political ideologies, in particular Marxism–Leninism. The system when I was there was anarchy mitigated by tribal loyalties and the dictates of gangs and militias, but the political mind-set of Marxism seemed to have remained entirely intact.

In the preceding months the political balance between the forces constituting what authority there was in Somalia had been shifting in subtle but significant ways. In retrospect I was fortunate to be there at that time, several months before the bungled American incursion, and to observe the political realities responsible for most of the famine conditions.

After spending several days discovering the mixed blessings of life in a state of anarchy, first in Mogadishu and then in Baidoa three hours away along a deteriorating bitumen road, and again back in Mogadishu, I felt I had a rudimentary understanding of what was entailed—the infrastructure of society destroyed down to and including basics like electricity, telephone, mail and just about every other public utility you can think of, and of course the law non-existent. And yet people carried on with their lives, went about their work, walked to the market place where you could buy not only fresh food but short-wave radios and the batteries to run them, rudimentary medical and sanitary supplies, all sorts of stuff, purchasable with foreign currency and even local currency (if you had a sack of it with you), or by barter. A substantial hospital, which I was shown through, was operating on power supplied by its own generators. There was a kind of natural order to life in the streets, though certainly no imposed order. I had a new respect for Peter Kropotkin. He was correct, anarchy *can* have its own order. Also, since a good number of men went about armed in one way or another, if you were inclined to rob someone you'd be thinking twice, because maybe they'd pull a gun or knife and kill you. Hence a kind of Hobbesian–Kropotkinism, I decided, gave anarchy its best shot: the threat of death, but from the armed citizen, not the state.

I'd read something about the United Somali Congress (USC) before leaving home. It was largely based on the Hawiye clan but had split, the stronger half being headed by General Mohamed Farrah Aidid based in South Mogadishu, about whom much more below. Before I ever walked into their headquarters I had already had tangential contact with them. I'd made friends with an extremely attractive CARE employee, a former stewardess with the defunct national carrier Somali Airlines, and she was sitting right beside me when I went in an armoured CARE vehicle to see the wrecked centre of the city. I got out and was taking photographs in the square in front of Mogadishu Cathedral when I was approached out of nowhere by a boy of about fourteen carrying an assault rifle and demanding my camera. I was arguing with him when an older youngster walked out of an adjacent building carrying a pistol, told the boy to lower his weapon and ordered me to clear out. This was USC territory, he explained, and they would not tolerate "spies." He had a point—it *had* been contested ground and might soon be again. I still had my camera.

We drove back to our compound, where the stewardess told me airline jokes. "What does Alitalia stand for?" "I don't know—Italia Wings?" "No. Always late in take-off and late in arrival." "Right …" "And what does Lufthansa stand for?" "No idea." "Let us fuck the hostesses as no stewards around." "OK, and they're good, I'll give you that. Got any more?" She had a dozen. I liked her a lot. Every morning she'd turn up in a different spotless dress, in fact I never met anyone grubbily dressed in Mogadishu. There was obviously some sort of water supply, perhaps from wells about the city.

It had been a lousy week for General Aidid, and this is where things get complicated, certainly far more complicated than represented in *Blackhawk Down*. Wanting to farewell visiting Irish President Mary Robinson, Aidid had been prevented from entering the airport in south Mogadishu by the armed gangs that the aid agencies paid to provide "security" there—and Aidid was supposed to be the man who controlled south Mogadishu. That was embarrassing enough. A few days later he learned that the Somali National Alliance (SNA) that he had stitched together out of his half of the United Somali Congress (USC), the Somali Sovereign National Movement (SSNM, a non-secessionist subset of the Somali National Movement of Northern Somalia which had seceded to become the Somaliland Republic), the Somali Democratic Movement (SDM), and the Somali Patriotic Movement (SPM, based on the Ogadeni clan), had just fallen apart in the southern port of Kismayu. The alliance was a praiseworthy effort to put together some sort of multi-clan structure to begin to govern a large part of the country, and it had considerable public support. It reflected well on Aidid.

I knew about some of this from our contacts, and it stimulated my curiosity. I decided to go and have a talk with the USC myself and see what I could learn at first-hand. The CARE Toyota Land Cruiser in which I was taken to the USC's Mogadishu headquarters was manned by a machine-gunner and two other guards with Kalashnikovs—without a vehicle so equipped a Westerner would not normally venture anywhere in Mogadishu or Somalia generally, although my Somali Airlines friend had walked me around the big marketplace with no guards accompanying us. In the USC compound I found the young Mr Abdi Haji Gobdon, Aidid's Director-General of Information, who turned out to be a genial host, very likeable I thought. He was particularly pleased to learn that I was not a journalist and that I was interested in political philosophy. Intellectuals, he said, were appreciated by the higher echelon of the USC, many of whom were themselves intellectuals.

"All these journalists," he told me (and he was surely right in this), "they're interested only in *actualité*, current events, no one has ever come here to talk to us about our political philosophy. General Aidid would be most interested to talk to you about that. Unfortunately he's not here at present."

"I see. Well, it's very nice to be able to talk with you, at least. Thank you. Actually, I'm hoping to see the General the day after tomorrow, in company with the President of CARE. From what I've read, the General's an interesting man." Words to that effect.

"You may be able to help him", Mr Gobdon thought. "When he was Siad Barre's ambassador to India he wrote a book on political philosophy. It's still unpublished. Ask him—he'll show it to you. Perhaps you can advise him where he might publish it."

"I'll do that if I get the chance", I replied. Siad Barre was the overthrown President and dictator, and Aidid had served as his ambassador to India in the 1980s.

"You wouldn't have some political literature, by any chance?" I asked him. "I'd like to take it away and study it."

He went inside and produced several roneoed editions of the *Daily News Bulletin* of SONNA, the Somali National News Agency. I opened one and glanced through a couple of paragraphs on the spot:

> Chairman Aidid gave [Ugandan] President Musaveni and his delegation a report on how Manifesto Group became to existence, how its existence created divisionism and other problems in the country, and its ties with Siad Barre and his henchmen … Siad Barre and his puppets, the ramshackle Manifesto Group, would shoulder the responsibility of the losses caused by the destructive civil war that depleted the country's economy, adding that the devotees of the SNA struggle had punished the Dictator Barre's culprits and crime perpetrators as well as his place-men (Manifesto Group) according to their deserts … Chairman Aidid who spoke to the huge gathering first greeted the thousands of joyous people who gathered there with their faces wreathed in smiles …

I was intrigued by some of Mr Gobdon's language here, or rather Aidid's, which Gobdon was reporting. "Divisionism," "henchmen," "puppets," "place-men," "culprits," "crime perpetrators"—it was the kind of Marxist–Leninist vocabulary one might have expected from the former regime, not from its enemies, but then most of its enemies were former members of Siad Barre's government. Obviously General Aidid's people were on a not dissimilar philosophical road, but one exemplifying more science, reflected here, I supposed, in Aidid's speech with its crystal-clear cause-and-effect structure and sharp categories.

"What's your own history?" I asked Mr Gobdon, thinking that almost all the younger intellectuals and politicals here had grown up under the influence of the old ideology. They'd been taught for twenty years to regard any sort of political opposition as "divisionism" and to demonise their political enemies, as Trotsky had demonised his, and Stalin his.

"I was a senior official in the Ministry of Information under Siad Barre," he replied. "Before that I was responsible for the Somali program on Radio Moscow." I told him I had sometimes listened to Radio Moscow on my SONY short-wave radio. I didn't say that Radio Moscow had long since abandoned the kind of vocabulary he and his friends were still using. In fact from my experience its vocabulary had been normal since I first listened-in during the early 1960s, unlike what one routinely heard on Radio Peking.

Two days later, after only four days' warning in which to fortify it, General Aidid's south-western stronghold of Bardera, a major aid centre, succumbed to a dawn attack by armed units aligned with the Somali National Front (SNF) and led by the cultivated General Mohammed Said Hersi Morgan, formerly Minister of Defence under ousted dictator Siad Barre. Morgan was Barre's son-in-law, reputedly the worst war criminal in the country, and known as the Butcher of Hargeisa. I relished the romantic Caribbean associations of his name but, from what I'd read, if one had to choose between a city's fate being in the hands of Morgan or Aidid, any well-disposed person would choose Aidid. And as soon as Morgan had captured Bardera from Aidid's forces he was already committing atrocities there, as we learned later.

It was just three hours after Aidid's loss of this town to Morgan that Malcolm Fraser as President of CARE International and CARE Australia's director Ian Harris met with an understandably edgy Aidid. I was also invited to attend and took detailed notes.

Aidid's personal compound in south Mogadishu was heavily guarded. You climbed to an upstairs landing and entered his private rooms, but first you removed your shoes, and once inside you sat on cushions, not chairs. This was the Islamic aspect of Aidid's USC. The rival USC led by the smooth Ali Mahdi Muhammad, self-styled "Interim President" and former hotelier, who held north Mogadishu and not much else and was coded under the term "Manifesto Group" in Aidid's propaganda, made no attempt to create any such effect. Like Aidid, Ali Mahdi belonged to the Hawiye clan, but to the Abgal branch, not Aidid's Habr Gedir branch. Through 1991 they had fought a civil war through Mogadishu itself, leaving this white-and-pale-blue, once-elegant Italian colonial city looted and in ruins. A "green line" separated its north from its south. You could still see how attractive it had been in colonial times, for the built environment of that period was entirely intact, including an arch of victory—interestingly, I found no resentment of Italy among the Somalis I met, or Russia for that matter, but on the other hand considerable anti-American feeling. The principal European destination of Somali Airlines when it was still flying had been Rome. It was a very different colonial experience from that of Ethiopia, though not from that of pro-Italian Eritrea. With the exception of British Somaliland to the north, Somalia in fact was under Italian administration until 1960.

Though Aidid and Ali Mahdi each theoretically controlled his half of the city, most of the arms with which the Soviet Union had flooded the country in the 1960s and 1970s were now in the hands of independent clan gangs, and neither leader seemed to exert much authority in the streets beyond his compound.

Aidid couldn't have guessed that we already knew about the fall of Bardera, from where one of CARE's aid workers, Bob Allen, had radioed us that he and two brave front-line journalists were hostages of the SNF. After handshakes all round, we received a history lesson designed to show that the chaos was everyone's fault but Aidid's. I already knew this from the SONNA newsletters, of course. Aidid told us he would never sit down with the man he had overthrown, the evil Siad Barre and his gang. Nor would he talk to the "Interim President" and his Manifesto clique until Ali Mahdi ceased calling himself "President." Aidid assured us he controlled eleven of the eighteen regions of Somalia. If only that had been true, the country may have been the better for it, for then more of the aid would have been getting through to the people who needed it, instead of into the hands of independent gangs. He told us he was reconciled to the 500 UN troops in Mogadishu, employed mainly at the docks, but not to the 3500 recently authorised by the Security Council—he would not tolerate such an infringement of Somali sovereignty. On and on it went. His evident inner strength contrasted with his diminutive and delicate appearance. His lieutenants beside him looked tough and supercilious.

"I'm sorry, General," Fraser interrupted, "but I have to contradict you."

Aidid was visibly put out. " … If you would permit me to continue?"

"Look, General, you don't even control your own centres. Two-and-a-half hours ago your forces were pushed out of Bardera. Now we hear that Morgan's men, victorious there, are closing on Sacco Uen [Sakow]. CARE thought it was safe in Bardera because it was *your* town, General, but our confidence was misplaced. As for your "control" here in Mogadishu, it's obviously not you who controls the streets of south Mogadishu but undisciplined gangs. Just listen to the random gunfire—it's totally *in*secure here. You don't even control the airport—right now the strip's closed because of clan fighting." (He wasn't callous enough to remind Aidid of the embarrassing incident with the Irish President.)

It was entirely true. In 1992 everyone in Somalia knew that the gangs of south Mogadishu were out of Aidid's control.

The General squinted through all of this in obvious agitation and I felt sorry for him.

"Please, sir! Please! If you would permit me to respond? First, it is true that we have been forced out of Bardera. I am sending reinforcements and we will retake that town, I assure you …"

"But, General, you had four days' warning of the attack and still you lost it."

"And we will re-take it, I promise you." This was no idle boast: subsequently Aidid's forces pushed Morgan right down to the Kenyan border.

"And then your point about security in Mogadishu", Aidid continued. "I am giving orders that all the armed gangs are to be forced off the streets and disarmed …"

"When, General? When will you do all this?"

"Within one week!"

Anybody in town with an appreciation of the situation on the streets would have known this was fantasyland.

Aidid also told us that he'd be prepared to talk with Ali Mahdi if the latter's absurd claim to be "Interim President" were first abandoned, but this was nothing new.

It was crystal clear from this interview that any suggestion of a negotiating table including seats for Siad Barre's "puppets", namely Morgan, which Aidid thought for a moment Fraser might be suggesting, was insulting to the suffering Somali people, of whom he was apparently the sole legitimate spokesman. General Morgan and the SNF should be wiped out—and would be. But Fraser wasn't suggesting any compromise with Morgan, just an exchange of intelligence with Aidid about the situation in Bardera and the fate of the hostages, about which Aidid seemed as much in the dark as we were, and certainly not placed to mediate.

The meeting was over. I decided not to ask Aidid about his political philosophy. No doubt there was intellectual substance behind it, but time was short because we were off to see Aidid's rival and Morgan's pal, Ali Mahdi, on the other side of the green line.

"What are we supposed to call him?" Fraser wondered as we climbed up to his office. "Mr President?"

"How about Excellency?" I suggested.

"That covers a nice range of sins ..."

In contrast to the Spartan frugality of Aidid's quarters, which I liked, Ali Mahdi's plush abode predisposed me against him. I could imagine that the Americans might prefer him, simply because he exuded softness and corruptibility. His sprawling carpeted office sat on the top of its building, the furniture a mixture of vulgarised Louis XV and soft velour-covered couches. When the old dictator Barre was losing his grip on the country Ali Mahdi was disparagingly referred to as the Mayor of Mogadishu. Now he was being referred to as the Mayor of *north* Mogadishu. The size of his entourage was impressive, and some of his guards actually wore uniforms. The Italians were apparently funding him to some extent, though it was said that they also had a little on Aidid, as one would. His enemies accused him of being in league with the old regime despite the fact that his Manifesto group had opposed Barre in 1990 and that its forces, not Aidid's, had taken Mogadishu from Barre. Many of his group were businessmen, which was held against him, "businessmen" being a dirty word in the vocabulary of Aidid's USC.

There was more than a little in the charge of collaboration thrown by Aidid against Ali Mahdi. Late in 1991 Ali Mahdi's section of the USC had held secret discussions with Morgan's SNF which boasted the remnant forces of Barre. After he lost Mogadishu, Barre had regrouped around Baidoa, causing immense havoc there, levelling unfriendly villages, poisoning dams, dynamiting wells and looting food stores, so that farmers were forced to eat their seed grains. It was actions like those, and the civil war more generally, that caused the famine, not so much drought, of which there is little in Somalia. Barre subsequently fled into exile in Nigeria but still had strong support among his own Marehan clan, and his son-in-law Morgan headed four or five thousand well-trained, well-equipped troops who seemed to be getting a lot of help from Kenya, an American ally.

One needed to know something about Barre because he was threatening to return through the agency of his son-in-law Morgan. Barre had taken power through a coup in 1969, nine years after the old Italian Somalia and British Somaliland fused to become independent Somalia. His Somali Socialist Revolutionary Party (SSRP), of which he was Secretary-General, had been set up in 1976 on Marxist–Leninist lines with advice from Moscow and East Berlin. There was a Politburo and a Central Committee that Barre chaired.

In the teeth of Somalia's intensely-felt and continually-fragmenting clan structures, Barre had attempted to obliterate "clanism" (read "human nature" in Somalia) through high-handed indoctrination teams known as victory pioneers, though his own power base was itself clan-centred (Marehan, with some Ogadeni and Dolbahante input). Revolutionary terror was considered a necessary weapon in this fight.

Barre's troubles had begun with his most popular action, the invasion of Ethiopia in 1977 to annex the Ethiopian part of the Ogaden desert. Overnight his Soviet support vanished—forced to choose between two client states, Moscow chose Ethiopia. The war ended in defeat. Blame attached to Barre, and through the late 1980s the loose clan alliance shoring him up fell apart. Meanwhile, with the end of the Cold War the Americans, who had to some extent replaced the Soviets as a foreign presence, lost interest too. Whatever strategic significance

Somalia once enjoyed was reduced to zero. Nobody any longer cared what happened there.

Barre had resisted pressure for political reform until it was too late. The battles he had fought as he retreated, first out of Mogadishu and then out of south-western Somalia generally, together with the civil war fought by his would-be successors in 1991, produced the universal ruin and anarchy I was witnessing.

On the morning we spoke with Ali Mahdi there just happened to be a delegation in the building from the SNF, in other words from Morgan, yet when we spoke about the fall of Bardera, now four hours past, Ali Mahdi pretended to be surprised. However, he promised to use his influence with Morgan and to send a high-level representative on the plane we were organising to fly down to Bardera to try to evacuate the expatriates. He also told us that the first thing he would put on the table at any reconciliation conference the UN might chair would be his surrender of the "Interim Presidency." In all this he seemed reasonable.

Later that morning we had closed discussions with the UN military commander, Pakistani Brigadier-General Imtiaz Shaheen, who the previous day had frankly spelt out for us his requirements beyond the inadequate 500 troops the UN had so far given him, and his frustrations with the slow UN bureaucracy. In the second meeting he told Fraser that in order to impress Morgan and the SNF in Bardera into releasing the hostages, a senior military man should go on the plane, and promptly nominated himself. He then flew down with E. K. Krishnan, CARE's director for Somalia, and a representative from Morgan's friend Ali Mahdi, and brought the expatriates out. This was not widely known. Shaheen was a man of initiative, but he turned out to be wrong in his belief that Aidid was bluffing in his loudly proclaimed resistance to further UN troops. Bloody events in 1993 would subsequently show how serious

Aidid was about the matter, as the Pakistanis and the Americans would learn to their cost.

Most of the food aid coming into Mogadishu by air and sea would be loaded onto trucks, many of which would then disappear, turning left or right at an intersection instead of rolling straight on to the intended destination. The food would go into some warehouse from where it would be sold off by profiteers and gangsters. That was one reason more UN troops were needed, in order to shepherd food convoys to their proper destinations. We found the same thing happening three hours west in Baidoa, at the centre of the famine.

For strategic reasons our attention now shifted there. It was the base town for a range of aid agencies including CARE, which had seven Australians comprising the majority of its expatriate staff at the town. CARE had intelligence that Morgan might at any time drive on Baidoa, ten hours by road from Bardera. Indeed a day later Morgan proclaimed its capture as his next war aim. So we flew to Baidoa by a six-seater light aircraft. I can't recall all six, but they included Fraser, Ian Harris, Tony Eggleston and myself.

Heroic efforts by CARE and others in this unsavoury town had saved thousands of lives. Efficient feeding centres, and the elementary medical care they provided, had turned the tide against famine here for the thousands of diseased and dying who were flooding in from the surrounding countryside. Phoebe Fraser was an effective team leader and coordinated everything. Richard Chambers, the Australian water engineer in Baidoa, had located the two bore-drilling machines still functioning in Somalia and restored many of the wells and drilled new ones. Looting was a major problem, though far less so than in Mogadishu. Twenty or more per cent of the airlifted food was going astray in Baidoa, but at least that ended up on the market where grain prices had fallen dramatically.

There was occasional random gunfire. Half the time it came from directly outside the compound. Was it intended to back up the demands of the drivers who were inside negotiating for more money? There was a pervading sense of menace but it never took concrete shape. Lockton Morrissey, the young ex-Army distribution co-ordinator, had a death threat hanging over him just because he was a tough negotiator and co-ordinator. Looking at the dispassionate gunmen in the streets, who couldn't care less, the drivers and truck owners who were forever upping their claims, the landlord who, not content with the US$1000 rent CARE was paying him, was now demanding $1500 for the use of his building, citing fellow rack-renters who were demanding $3000 from "their" agencies, anyone not yet cynical about human nature would wisen up.

The ambush story Lockton told me was unbeatable. The elders of a village had complained to him that the convoy of trucks bringing tons of grain to their village had never arrived. It had come part of the way up the road, then turned off and disappeared, obviously to sell the load somewhere or other. Lockton, previously an officer in an elite Australian Army unit, planned a strategy.

"We're sending another convoy to you tomorrow. It's your food. You ambush it. I'll show you how."

He directed their village gunmen to set up a roadblock closer in to Baidoa, just before the turnoff down which the trucks had disappeared. Then, when the convoy halted, others blocked its retreat from the rear. At gunpoint they forced the unloading of every truck to the last bag of grain and transferred everything to their own vehicles, bringing it safely to their warehouse.

On my last night in Baidoa, and in Somalia, we were bent over a large map of the country. Fraser was for taking advice he'd received from General Shaheen and evacuating completely, while CARE's Somalia director favoured leaving a skeleton staff. Fraser asked Lockton for a threat assessment.

Indicating the main road from Bardera and alternative tracks around it, Lockton pointed out that if Morgan was so inclined, he could have his advance units in Baidoa right now. Before his main force arrived, however, there'd be an enormous battle somewhere on the road from Bardera. Aidid's men—and it was they who would be our hope—would concentrate an opposition, but if they lost they'd fall back through Baidoa demoralised and desperate. A dispirited and defeated army is more dangerous to civilians than a victorious army.

"They'll go after fuel, they'll go after vehicles, they'll go after food. There's only one source and that's us. Maybe they'll take hostages too."

So we flew south into Kenya the next day and I was glad to be out of there. Somalia needed order, and democracy was low in its hierarchy of needs. Abdi Gobdon had been right about divisionism, it was Somalia's curse, but who was to command? As forces manoeuvred and alliances were shifting, Fortune favoured the most ruthless. We needn't have worried, however. Morgan's forces would soon be in retreat and the roads as far as the Kenyan border would be Aidid's, for the time being.

Friendship out of enmity: Ian Paisley (right) with his deputy Martin McGuinness (ex-Provisional Sinn Fein). "I can go down to Dublin now and be well received there", Paisley told the author. Irish Times.

10

Afternoon Tea with Ian Paisley

In October 2011, thirty-nine years after Ulster's Bloody Sunday massacre of 1972, nineteen years after the collapse of the 1992 peace talks between Catholics and Protestants, chaired by Sir Ninian Stephen, thirteen years after the Good Friday Agreement of 1998 finally brought peace to Northern Ireland, I flew to Dublin *en route* to Belfast to interview Ian Paisley, former First Minister of Northern Ireland and leader of the Democratic Unionist Party (DUP), as part of research into Stephen's life and work.[33] I'm using the terms Ulster and Northern Ireland without any preference. They have different flavours. Protestants often prefer the first, Catholics the second.

I'd written to Paisley from Australia and was in telephone and email communication with his second daughter Rhonda, who was acting

33 For an account of the peace talks conducted by Sir Ninian Stephen in 1992 see Chapter 7, "No Surrender in Ulster", in the author's *Fortunate Voyager: The Worlds of Ninian Stephen* (Miegunyah/Melbourne University Press, Carlton, 2013), pp. 151–166.

as his secretary. Rhonda Paisley is an artist noted for her paintings of still life, interiors and landscapes, mostly in a *naïf* style, and she is a longstanding and active member of her father's political party. She is also a former Lady Mayoress of Belfast.

Like her father, Rhonda was outspoken in the Unionist cause—too outspoken, saying what she thought instead of what might have been considered appropriate. For example, on 28 July 1991, at a time when the British Government was engaging with representatives of the Irish Republic on a transition towards peace in the North, a Protestant paramilitary outfit, the Ulster Freedom Fighters (UFF), armed with plastic explosives, headed south across the border and carried out a series of incendiary bombings of shops in the Republic. On the following day, when asked by reporters for her view of these events, Rhonda Paisley said the bombings were "perfectly understandable" in the light of the "betrayal" of Ulster being carried out by the British and Republican Governments. She would have done better to prevaricate. A hostile press on both sides of the religious divide, editorialising on behalf of the public as they do, condemned her. The offence was considered particularly deplorable given her position as a DUP councillor on Belfast's city council. Not that she was necessarily an obedient member of the DUP. Fourteen years later, in 2005, she pursued a legal action against the party, naming her father into the bargain, for what she claimed was discrimination against her when she was turned down for a policy-and-communications position within the party.

When I left Melbourne for Europe to investigate aspects of Stephen's youth, including his schooling in Switzerland, Rhonda had not yet finalised the details of when and where I would meet her father. It might be in London at Westminster, where he sat in the House of Lords as Lord Bannside, or it might be at his home in Belfast. She said she'd let me know closer to the week we'd tentatively agreed on. This was why I hadn't booked airline tickets for the Belfast leg of my itinerary prior to leaving Australia. I installed myself for a few weeks in the vacant house of friends, in the medieval Italian village of Massino Visconti, high up over Lake Maggiore, but it wasn't there that I received the finalised details from Rhonda, it was in Switzerland over lunch at a lakeside restaurant in Montreux.

I seemed to be researching Ninian Stephen's life simultaneously from each end, which works with bridges and conforms with the B-theory of time. I'd driven from Stresa up through Domodossola and across the Swiss border, then down the Simplon Pass onto Route 9 westbound through the Rhone valley to Montreux. As I drove I kept checking my iPhone for emails from Rhonda. Just above Montreux, in the village of Glion, was where Stephen had attended the last of his schools prior to coming to Australia in 1940 at he age of sixteen. This was Chillon College. I already knew something about his time there, mainly from him, but I wanted to see it for myself and discover whether any institutional records had survived. Privately owned and expensive Swiss schools like Chillon College tend to change hands every decade or two, and when they finally close, as most now have, the last owner is not always diligent about preserving records. I met with the last owner's son, who in 2011 owned the private school Indira Gandhi attended at Montreux in the 1930s (under a different owner). As far as he knew, all the records of Chillon College died with his father, if they survived that long. In any case the owner in Stephen's time had been someone else. After driving up the serpentine road from Montreux to Glion I could see how exhilarating, and dangerous, it would have been to luge down that same road, as Stephen frequently did when it was covered in ice and snow in the winter of 1938–39, though with fewer cars to get in the way. I opened the door, got out and walked around the outside of the big building. All of its windows were shuttered, its doors were locked and it stood silent in its treed park. No files or records of anything inside there, just ghosts of the past. I strolled through the park and exposed a roll of 6X6 transparencies on a 1939 Rolleidoscop. Montreux was spread out below and the lake stretched to the mountains on the far side.

While standing there I checked my emails: *still* nothing from Rhonda. The contrast between this tranquil place and the violent history of Ulster was matched by the difference in temperament between the two men. Stephen was an agnostic and sceptic who took a cool and disinterested view of most things. Paisley was an uncompromising fundamentalist on the edge of righteous anger. No wonder Stephen found him the most difficult participant in the talks. Yet he had told me how much he enjoyed Paisley's company away from the round-table disagreements. Lady Stephen said the same. I'd first talked to them about Paisley in 1993, at the home of mutual friends, the Hossacks, soon after they'd returned to Australia from the talks. Stephen told me he had invited the various delegations to dinner, each on a separate occasion, and how that helped—and helped *him* understand *them*. I asked him his impression of Paisley, and his answer was "I liked him". Paisley, he said, had tremendous presence, his strong views were put forcefully, but while he could be very difficult he also could be charming. So I was looking forward to meeting the man.

I drove back down into Montreux, parked by the lake and walked into the grounds of the *Restaurant Terrasse Safran* where you can dine outdoors, just along from the 1906 Montreux Palace Hotel with its stunning yellow awnings, where Vladimir Nabokov lived for the last sixteen years of his life after *Lolita* relieved him of having to live on an American college professor's income. I sat down at an empty table, ordered a cocktail, studied the menu and re-checked my phone. Pleasant surprise—there *was* something from Rhonda: we could meet at their family home in East Belfast the following Tuesday afternoon. I ordered seafood and sent her a reply, accepting the date, then called my travel agent in Australia, where it was night, leaving a message to book a return ticket on Aer Lingus departing Milan for Dublin the following Monday and returning Wednesday.

On the Monday morning I flew out of Milan's Malpensa and overnighted in Dublin, hired a car and drove north on the M1/N1/A1 past Drogheda, Dundalk and across a border with no "Slow Down" signs, no barriers and no border police. Then Newry, Lisburn and on into central Belfast, east on Newtownards Road, south into Beersbridge Road and left into shady Cyprus Avenue, lined both sides with glorious lindens, Austrian pines and sycamores. The secluded houses along that avenue aren't grand or showy, they're quiet and private. Northern Ireland singer/songwriter Van Morrison wrote a song he titled "Cyprus Avenue" about a girl he knew who lived there. Not far away, in less enticing streets, I noticed a lot of Union Jacks, as you'd expect, but I saw none in Cyprus Avenue—perhaps considered naff by the residents there, or too blatant. The Paisley residence was the manse house of the Martyrs Memorial Church, part of the Free Presbyterian Church of Ulster established by Paisley himself. The house was bombed in 1973 but little damage was done to the fabric—extraordinary that it wasn't more closely guarded at the time, when Paisley had recently been elected to the House of Commons as MP for North Antrim.

I knew sufficient for my purposes about the man who lived there. In theological terms he represented the most uncompromising strand of hard-line Calvinist Presbyterianism, undiluted by the four-and-a-half centuries since John Knox. Paisley's view of the Roman Catholic Church was identical to that of Knox, and of John Bunyan in his seventeenth-century allegorical novel *The Pilgrim's Progress*: the Pope—the Bishop of Rome—is the Antichrist incarnate or at least *an* Antichrist, and his corrupted institution, the Roman Catholic Church, is the Whore of Babylon, seated on the Seven Hills and drunk with the blood of the true Christians she's martyred. You may have seen such images in *Awake* and *Watchtower*, if you take those magazines. It's all laid out in the Book of Revelation. The Church of Rome, according to traditional Protestantism, was never universal—the Eastern churches were as old—and had derailed herself somewhere or other in the early Dark Ages, it's hard to say when. Ever since, it makes war upon the true Church, upon the Lamb of God and His faithful followers, persecuting and martyring them. Thus there could be no compromise with Popery, which, under the banners of James II's army, failed to crush the Protestant defenders of Londonderry in 1689 and would just love to try it on again. That meant the maintenance of a strong and armed defence on behalf of the Protestant majority in Ulster; rejection of any attempt by the British Government to coerce Ulster into a compromise with the Irish Republic ("Ulster will fight, and Ulster will be right" was a slogan); and opposition to the agendas of the Catholic minority in the North, who naturally had a different view and had been pressing for equal rights and fair elections since the early 1960s.

Paisley's theology was neither good nor bad, since theology (like philosophy) is non-empirical, not developing in any agreed sense. Hard-line Calvinism was traditional and vigorous in that little world, and out of it came the politics of the party Paisley founded, the Democratic Unionist Party, which had grown into the dominant party of Ulster. In the early 1990s with the first hesitant moves by Westminster and Dublin towards multilateral negotiations on possible power-sharing arrangements for Northern Ireland, the historical past was still very much alive in the present. How long the impasse between the sides was sustainable was one question, another was connected with it: how long before the Catholics in the North would outbreed the Protestants? The only conceivable peaceful solution *was* power-sharing, which was what the talks Sir Ninian Stephen chaired in 1992 were intended to facilitate.

I also knew that Paisley had a fifty-year history as a firebrand. He'd been jailed for his political activities on the riotous streets of Ulster and had worn that as a badge of pride. In 1968, following a wave of attacks by Protestant paramilitaries on Catholic houses supposedly belonging to adherents of the IRA, Paisley was reported to have told loyalists that "Catholic homes caught fire because they were loaded with petrol bombs. Catholic churches were attacked and burned because they were arsenals and priests handed out sub-machine guns to parishioners". In 1969 he was reported to have told a loyalist rally that the Catholics of Northern Ireland "breed like rabbits and multiply like vermin". "Save Ulster from Sodomy" was one of his campaign slogans through the 1970s and 80s when he fought against the legalisation of homosexuality. In 1979 he was elected to the European Parliament, and in 1988, when Pope John Paul II addressed its members, Paisley stood up and loudly abused him: "I denounce you, Antichrist! I refuse you as Christ's enemy and Antichrist, with all your false doctrine!" Years earlier, on the death of Pope John XXIII, Paisley summed him up in nine words: "This Romish man of sin is now in Hell".[34] I was hoping to hear some of this sort of language first-hand, in fact I couldn't wait to experience it.

One of the extraordinary things I'd learned about Paisley was that back in 1981 he had created his own militia, Ulster's Third Force (UTF), supplementing other Protestant paramilitary units (Ulster Volunteer

34 "The Sayings of Ian Paisley", *The Irish Times*, 5 March 2008.

Force, Ulster Freedom Fighters, Ulster Defence Association, Red Hand Commando), all formed to do battle with the dominant Catholic militia, the Provisional IRA (the non-Marxist offshoot from the old and much-declined regular IRA). The proximate cause of Paisley's creation of the UTF had been the Ulster-related talks then going on between the Thatcher Government and Charles Haughey's Government in Dublin. On a starry moonless night on 6 February 1981 Paisley brought together on a hillside in County Antrim five hundred men, all brandishing their shooters' licences, and lined them up in formation. Reporters were there by his invitation. These men, Paisley declared, were "a small token of the men who are placed to devastate any attempt by Margaret Thatcher and Charles Haughey to destroy the Union", adding "I will take full responsibility for anything these men do. We will stop at nothing."[35] When Bunyan wrote in praise of "the warfaring Christian" he was thinking of spiritual warfare. Paisley had in mind the purchase of weapons as the next step. Over the following months there were more night-time rallies. Thousands of masked and uniformed men paraded before him at an East Belfast rally on 23 November 1981. All of them, he announced, were "ready to be recruited under the crown to destroy the vermin of the IRA. But if they refuse to recruit them, then we will have no other decision to make but to destroy the IRA ourselves."[36] The UTF, or at least many of its recruits, subsequently merged with the Ulster Resistance and were armed with the latest Czechoslovakian Vz58 assault rifles and rocket-propelled grenades.

But times change, and with them, sometimes, the men of violence. A few years after the Good Friday Agreement Paisley did finally accept the historical inevitability of a power-sharing arrangement for Northern

35 David McKittrick, *Through the Minefield* (Blackstaff Press, Belfast, 1996), p. 46.
36 Michael Hall, *The Death of the Peace Process?* (Island Publications, Newtownabbey, 1997), p. 10.

Ireland. In 2004, on behalf of the DUP, he discussed this in London with Irish Prime Minister Bertie Ahern. It turned out that Paisley was gravely ill at the time, and that's perhaps relevant, because the prognosis was death.

Deals were done with the political wing of the Provisional IRA, Sinn Fein, and with its leader Gerry Adams. On 8 May 2007 Westminster devolved power to Northern Ireland: Paisley, now strengthening in health, was elected First Minister of Northern Ireland, and Sinn Fein's Martin McGuinness was elected as Paisley's Deputy First Minister. The two established an excellent working relationship and became friends. On taking his seat at Stormont as First Minister of Northern Ireland Paisley said the following:

> I have sensed a great sigh of relief amongst all our people who want the hostility to be replaced with neighbourliness. The great King Solomon said: "To everything there is a season, and a time to every purpose under heaven. A time to be born and a time to die. A time to plant and a time to pluck up that which is planted. A time to kill and a time to heal. A time to break down and a time to build up. A time to get and a time to lose. A time to keep and a time to cast away. A time to love and a time to hate. A time of war and a time of peace."
>
> I believe that Northern Ireland has come to a time of peace, a time when hate will no longer rule.[37]

In 2011 when I was walking into Paisley's garden, this was in the recent past. He'd since retired from active politics in Ulster and Westminster but was still sitting in the House of Lords as a life peer.

I walked around by the side of the house, uncertain of where the main entrance was, when Rhonda evidently noticed me and called me to the door. Paisley was eighty-five at the time and he still stood 6'5". He welcomed me and shook my hand. Rhonda and her mother Eileen were

[37] London *Telegraph*, 8 May 2007.

standing there too. They led me into a cosy and well-furnished living room, and Eileen Paisley asked would I like some tea. Dishonestly, I said I couldn't think of anything nicer. I knew I wouldn't be offered anything alcoholic in that house, since most Ulster Free Presbyterians are teetotal. After a few minutes' small talk Eileen Paisley and Rhonda appeared with trays bearing teapot, cups and saucers, as well as cakes and savouries. I realised by now that I wouldn't be interviewing Ian Paisley alone but also his wife and daughter, who had their own memories of the Stephens. I asked them if I could tape the conversations and they had no objections. In this line of work it's a necessity but I loathe doing interviews, I despise myself for digging into people's thoughts and feelings, it's parasitic, and most especially I hate hearing myself on the tape afterwards. It's not of me. Fortunately their memories needed little prompting.

"Sir Ninian was a very *straight* man", Paisley said at the outset, "and then, of course, the great thing about him was he wasn't in anybody's pocket. He made it clear he wasn't there to sell out Northern Ireland. He was one man who was above it all, and I was very fond of him. He was very honest, and he had a sympathy with the Ulster position. I had some very good times with him."

However, there were limits to how far the Democratic Unionist Party could go—or was prepared to go at that stage. "The great thing was to get us to go to Dublin, and I said 'No! Let them come to us, but we're not going to them, because that would be a surrender.'"

"It was too soon", Rhonda explained. Present through most of the talks, she thought they served an important purpose by opening the way to a settlement while closing no doors. "There was nothing in the talks that created a barrier to future talks, and if anything the opposite." She commented on what she saw as the sense of fairness in Stephen's procedures. "He treated them like grown-ups, instead of the children the British Government thought of them as."

"You could trust him", Paisley emphasised. "All sides trusted him. He never crossed anybody."

On the other hand it was clear that Paisley neither liked nor trusted Lord Mayhew, Secretary of State for Northern Ireland, the *éminence grise* behind the process, in particular because of what Paisley identified as Mayhew's instinct for control, frustrated by Stephen's complete independence.

"Sir Ninian couldn't be controlled by the British."

"The British Government was just another party to the talks", Rhonda added, "and those talks were significant, because it was the first time we'd ever been face-to-face around a table."

She recalled one meeting with Stephen in particular, following a serious leak. "The draft of a document was available, but you could only read that document in the room with him, the document had to be handed back to him, and I remember everybody was writing frantically to get a summary of it. Afterwards Sir Ninian said to Dad that he didn't like to handle a meeting like that because, even though there may only have been one or two leakers, he made them all feel like they weren't trusted, and he preferred not to do that."

In the wake of the talks, the Province endured a string of bloody actions by the paramilitaries but, as Paisley pointed out, Stephen "left a hope within people that we *could* negotiate. He certainly helped us on the right road. He came, worked very hard, did a good job."

Through the afternoon we talked about the changed situation in the wake of the Good Friday Agreement of 10 April 1998.

"I can go down to Dublin now", Paisley told me, "and be well received there." He also told me he was continuing on good terms with his former Deputy First Minister Martin McGuinness of Sinn Féin, who in his younger years had been a member of the Provisional IRA, who like Paisley has spent time in jail for his beliefs, who like Paisley is a total abstainer, and who at that moment was running for President of the Republic, though Northern Ireland is his home.

"There's been a generational change up here", he added, "and also in the South. Here the younger generation know nothing of the Troubles, down there they know nothing of the old Catholicism."[38]

"That can't be bad", I said.

"No, it can't."

We spent about three hours together, talking more generally as well. Before I left they gave me several books to take home with me. One of them was *Ian Paisley: A Life in Photographs.* Paisley took a pen and inscribed it: "Ian Paisley. Eph 6: 19 & 20". Later I looked up this passage in St Paul's Epistle to the Ephesians: "… that utterance may be given unto me, that I may open my mouth boldly, to make known the mystery of the gospel. For which I am an ambassador in bonds: that therein I may speak boldly, as I ought to speak."

The reference could be read as justifying his past actions and stances, but the kind of boldness that had landed him in jail and threatened violence had given way to a conciliatory frame of mind that he obviously enjoyed being in, and maybe that involved boldness too. In a sense I was disappointed. I'd looked forward to hearing the firebrand in full and violent rant but it was a time to put aside ranting and a time when his time was shortening.

38 Author's notes, tape recording and recollections from an afternoon with Ian, Eileen and Rhonda Paisley in Belfast, 4 October 2011.

11

Deceased but Undeparted

I thought of Charles as a contemporary though he was sixteen years my senior. He was young in the ways he thought and behaved, good looking for his age, immensely charming. When he was younger he'd been mistaken more than once for the actor Robert Cummings (*Dial M For Murder*). There was an unpredictability about him that made it exciting and conceivably just a little dangerous to be around him. He'd do odd things I'd never seen done before. For instance, I found, when we turned up at a restaurant, that he'd booked himself in under a different name—I wondered whether he carried credit cards in more than one name, as I'd seen done by someone close to me. When I asked why he did it he said it enabled him to book into a restaurant or hotel on a second occasion if he'd ruined his name by failing to turn up the first time, but I wasn't entirely convinced. Maybe there was something else to it.

He'd put together an anthology of short fiction for American college students. It made a lot of money for Prentice Hall and a decent cut for him. In a lecture hall filled with admiring students at a major east-coast university, where he headed the English Department for a time, he once let fire with a Smith & Wesson revolver loaded with blanks, in order to illustrate the psychological effect of violent action upon a group of people. It was relevant to the story he was discussing, Flannery O'Connor's *The Misfit.* One student rushed out of the lecture hall in a fit of fear to report his discomfort to the university authorities, but the rest remained seated. The incident was splashed all over the town's local paper, a copy of which Charles sent me, perhaps because he thought I'd admire him for it. What impressed me in the matter was his unconcern for his career, just as I'd be impressed by someone walking along the edge of a precipice. He kept his job only because his students rallied to his defence.

He enjoyed flouting liberal taboos, "liberal" in the American sense. For instance he once sent me a photograph of himself squatting beside a security firm's notice on the lawn of a friend's house in Palm Springs. It read "Armed Response." I asked him to get me one of those so I could put it on my own front lawn. The threat to kill any trespasser was latent in the ambiguity and entirely legal.

His grandfather was born in 1828, eight years before the Alamo, and was conscripted to fight for the Union in the War Between the States—he paid another to take his place, as you could if you had the money and the sense to steer away from the road of death. I found Charles's two-generational link to 1828 pretty impressive, though it's not all that remarkable: his grandfather must have been about fifty at the birth of Charles's father, who would have been around fifty when Charles was born. Anyway it was less impressive than the interplays of will and fate I associate with him. In the 1948 Max Ophüls film *Letter from an Unknown Woman* the Joan Fontaine character says at one point that "The course of our lives can be changed by such little things. So many passing by, each intent on his own problems. So many faces that one might easily have been lost. I know now that nothing happens by chance. Every moment is measured, every step is counted".

We became friends during the six-month period he spent as a Visiting Professor in Melbourne in 1989. He was living at the house of a colleague of mine, who was living for a few months in America, and he would invite me around to help him drink the in-house supplies of whisky he'd discovered in a cabinet at her place. It didn't take us long to get through it. We'd drive down to Cinema Point, eighty miles south-west, where I was living half the week in my friend Claudio Veliz's cliff-side house, South Main, during Claudio's first year heading the University Professors section of Boston University for its President, John Silber. South Main, as I've pointed out before, sits below the lookout there, just where the Great Ocean Road becomes really elevated, high up over spectacular ledges of rock across which the waves of the Southern Ocean ceaselessly crash. I prefer it in autumn and winter when the sense of loss permeates the place.

During the day we'd walk, Charles and I, the four-mile arc of beach from Cinema Point to Aireys Inlet and I'd tell him about shipwrecks that had occurred along this rocky coast in the nineteenth century—three months of sailing through tumultuous seas in patient anticipation of a new life, and then suddenly death by night. In the evenings we'd sit by the fire listening to the Velizes' opera recordings. I told him of a dread I had about that place. There's a point in *Rigoletto* where a storm is abating and a bell begins to sound. I'd dreamed that around 3.00 a.m., in the midst of a storm, the bell Claudio had rigged up outside the entrance door began to clang. How could it sound of itself? Who was there, and how had they found their way down the precipitous path in the pitch black?

We'd talk about American history and politics (he said he was a Republican), or a new novel he was working on. He'd published a successful historical novel for young people, but later novels had been rejected and lay about in drawers. He'd talk about the war and the time he'd spent on Okinawa shortly after the end of hostilities when he was seventeen. The island was still haunted by the spirits of the tens of thousands of non-combatant Japanese, many of them mothers with their babes, who had thrown themselves off cliffs to avoid capture by the Americans. The smell of death still hung about the place when he was there. He'd talk about those times, about his college years, about the women he'd known, and about his ex-wife. We never discussed religion—he wasn't interested, though his father had been a prominent Presbyterian minister in Wilmington and has a place in the *Dictionary of American Biography*. "When you're dead, you're dead" he assured me.

"Curious, though, what happened at the staff meeting the other day" I replied. One of the secretaries had asked me afterwards had I seen the woman in dark green sitting in the corner beside the bookshelves—when she looked again the woman was gone. I said I hadn't noticed her. I did know that a female student had jumped out of the windows there, six floors up.

Charles laughed. "She dozed and dreamed it."

There was something about him he wasn't letting on, beneath the run-of-the-mill talk, so on one occasion I manufactured an elaborate lure he wasn't dumb enough to take.

"I always thought that statement by the character in Chekhov's *The Lady With a Dog*, about one's real self being different from what the world sees, that that was pretty right, didn't you? That everything essential to you, the kernel of your life, is hidden from other people. It'd mean you couldn't take much account of what you see in others because everyone would have their real life under the cover of secrecy."

"You and me both", he replied. "It's true. We know we're defined not by the work we do, the people we work with or the things we write, but predominantly by something else. It might be an obsession, a vice, another person—whatever it was, we'd know it was pretty central in what defined us."

"OK, and if we're attached to whatever it is, do we take it with us when we leave?"

"Let's say we die into another world (though I don't believe we do). If they stole *that* from you it'd diminish *them*." By "them" I supposed he meant God.

So I still didn't know what "that" was, though if it was something he didn't wish to lose then it was valued and not despised. Certainly he never made a move on me that I noticed—and anyhow there was Joan.

He took a couple of weeks off for a rail trip to Perth on the trans-continental and sent me two postcards. The first, mailed just after he reached Perth, read "I was sitting on the train reading the *West Australian* when I saw a half-page advertisement: Australia's leading cosmetics consultant would be in Perth's Myer Department Store during the week to talk with women about their make-up. There was a photograph of her. I couldn't believe my eyes, because she was sitting across from me in the club car. I introduced myself and bought her a drink."

A couple of days later I received a second: "You won't believe it! I was on a tour around Perth and noticed the same honey-blonde woman from Melbourne sitting close by, so in obedience to fate I made a distinct move. Well, what *else* should I do? Tbc."

A fortnight after his return to Melbourne I got a call: "I'm taking her out, and I told her about you. She'd like to meet you. Come around this

Saturday night for dinner to her place down here at Mt Eliza."

So I turned up around 7.00 p.m. and parked in the garden. The evening was warm and the scent of honeysuckle hung in the air along the drive. I turned off the engine, got out and walked to the entrance at the back of the two-storeyed house—the reception rooms would be downstairs, with the front of the house looking out over the bay, down to which there'd be a private walking track, the standard thing in that little precinct. It was already night and the lights of the bayside suburbs clear around to the city thirty miles away reflected in the waters below.

Charles opened the door to me and led the way into the kitchen. There was a Strauss waltz, the Emperor, coming from a radio or tape player somewhere. "She's downstairs", he said. "I'm fixing some pre-dinner things. Help yourself to Scotch—there's ice in the bucket and soda in the siphon." I remember all this sharply and the words are close.

As I was complying I noticed a portrait on the wall.

"Is that her?" I asked, trying my drink, deciding it needed more ice and soda and acting on that.

"That's a portrait she had done by someone or other, yes."

The woman in the portrait was familiar—the facial features, especially the eyes, and the thick hair done up like that, very early-60s. I knew this woman from *some*where and she was waiting below.

"OK now", he instructed, "put your drink on this tray—you take the tray, I'll take the other stuff. We're going down."

As soon as I met Joan and heard her voice with its modulation and tonalities it clicked. Her voice was one of the best things about her.

In my time as an undergraduate in Adelaide in the early 1960s I'd occasionally killed time by walking across North Terrace and into the

David Jones department store, where I'd watched her. I'd watched her close-by, near enough to smell the perfume she was wearing, and I'd watched her from up on the mezzanine where they served coffee and cakes. A cappuccino cost three shillings and for ten you could have two of them and a slice of chocolate cake with clotted cream. Joan was Revlon's foremost beauty consultant at that time and for a good number of years thereafter. She'd also worked for Coty. Dressed to kill and impeccably made-up, typically she'd have a microphone in one hand as she introduced the latest product range and proceeded to supervise the makeover of some woman from among the crowd that inevitably gathered round.

Most of the women watching her always seemed over the hill to me. Obviously that was good from her point of view—more to work on, better before-and-after contrast, and they could afford the stuff. She achieved impressive results, and later it was clear from what she told me that she was widely respected in her field. Revlon would send her to Tokyo and other Asian cities to do this job, even around to Buenos Aires, pay her well and put her up in the best hotels. The crowd watching her invariably included a number of men, all of whom would have liked to go to bed with her. I was seventeen or eighteen and would've needed a couple of amphetamines, available free from my 24-hour pharmacist friend Warwick, before even thinking of asking her to join me for a drink after the show. I envied Charles his luck.

Joan seemed impressed by the details in my box of memories and told me straight out "I approve of Charles's choice of friend, Philip". "I love you too", I told her, "like I did back then". She was a widow of several years' standing and had the self-possession that allowed her to live happily alone, but I could see she'd fallen for Charles.

He returned to America a couple of months later but continued to see a lot of her. They'd meet each year for two or three weeks in London during what used to be called the Season and he'd take her to all the latest shows, something he'd been accustomed to indulge in for years. They'd also meet in Maui and in Maryland. The arrangement was that Joan would cover her own travel costs and he'd cover just about everything else. There were a lot of these trips. Given the spectacularly-sited house she lived in, he was assuming she must be rich, but it eventually became clear to him, through her own confession on one occasion, that all these trips were draining her cash reserves, and that night he confided in his diary "So I've discovered her secret, but she hasn't discovered mine."

When we die we leave behind our diaries, if we've kept any, and they lie around begging to be read as the only things that any longer speak for us. They speak for us but they can't answer, and the secret was beyond reach by the time Joan read those words.

"Do you have any idea what his secret was?" she asked me on one of our telephone conversations following his death.

"No, I don't", I told her honestly, "none of them, I only know my own. It must have been a big one for him to single it out like that. He never said anything that suggested what it could be. Maybe he sensed I'd be critical, though whatever it was I wouldn't have cared. I really have no idea."

But back to the narrative present. It wasn't long before they decided to get married, but on account of some insignificant heart murmur, Joan had trouble persuading the local American Consulate to grant her a residence visa for the United States. Ultimately it came through and she left to marry Charles and live with him at his principal house near his university, and on weekends at Rock Hall in Maryland, on the eastern shore. They also had a Queensland apartment at Noosa.

Meanwhile I'd instituted a literature course based around Charles's best-selling anthology. Although my field at that time was eighteenth-century English literature and culture, the Department had gone over to a smorgasbord-style choice of courses for the three-year major, with just two or three compulsory period courses, and I knew that if I didn't offer a popular course in modern literature I'd face the consequences of declining enrolments in my pre-1800 offerings. The worst consequence would be having to help some colleague teach an ideologically-committed course I instinctively disliked, maybe Marxist or radical feminist—there were a number of these and that was not going to happen to me. By this stage the world of the humanities was a place I was in but no longer of me. There were schools of this and that, with the constituent fields no longer disciplines, for they'd been infected by theories specifically designed to deprive them of stable meaning. Subsequently, being fortunate enough not to need to work any more, I retired early without any "package" incentive.

The best thing about Charles's anthology was that it came with a separate Instructor's Manual, not available to students, which contained his analysis of every single one of its hundred-odd short stories, as well as a concise bibliography for each one. I mined it unashamedly, as he suggested I do. After all, it wasn't my field. As he was about to retire from his university he gave me hundreds of slides related to the stories, and these made the course even more attractive. All our courses were advertised on a noticeboard down along the corridor and mine put the emphasis on "Short". I set out to compete with courses on the novel. "There are just fifty to sixty pages of reading a week in this course", my advert read, "but *close* reading". Not that I needed to salve their consciences. My notice had the desired effect: during the years in which I offered the course, an annual average of 160 students chose it, and I had to get a colleague to help me out by taking a couple of seminar groups. The then-head of department walked into one of the overcrowded seminars prior to my arrival one day and said to my students "Come on now, tell me honestly, you're only doing this course because the reading is *short*, aren't you?" Arriving in the room just as he was speaking, my question to him in front of all the students was "Why did you need to ask?"

In 1990, partly in order to work on the 3rd Earl of Burlington's Chiswick Villa library now at Chatsworth, I flew to London via Philadelphia and stayed with Charles, shortly before he married Joan, who still didn't have residency. His house was adjacent to the university grounds and we'd walk to his office past rows of enormous dead trees killed by Dutch Elm Disease and insensible to the breezes meant to cool them. He drove me into Pennsylvania, around the Amish area, through towns with odd names (Paradise, *via* Intercourse), and to a Revolutionary War battlefield on the Brandywine River where hundreds of rebels lie beneath the fields in mass graves dug by the victorious British. There's something tangible about the spirit of that unhappy place.

Three years later, in 1993, I was teaching at Vassar College, on the Hudson a couple of hours north of New York City. There were around 2,000 students enrolled at Vassar at that time, mostly young women but men as well—the place had recently become co-educational. The grounds included a large acreage of treed parks and lake-land. Vassar is one of the Ivy League's Seven Sisters and includes among its alumnae Jacqueline Bouvier (Kennedy Onassis), Jane Fonda, Meryl Streep, and Mary McCarthy who made the college the setting for her novel *The Group*. There's immense tradition but it's worn lightly.

On long weekends I'd drive down to be with Charles and Joan. The two-storeyed house was even more inviting than it had been three years earlier. The reception rooms and kitchen had been transformed, and breakfasts and other meals were a lot better than those Charles had formerly prepared for me.

"I've never felt so alive", he told me.

It was late October of 1993 and my son Julian had flown across to stay a few weeks with me. Naturally we were invited down by Charles and Joan to stay in their principal house and also on the Chesapeake Bay at Rock Hall, and we happily complied. Having already been there in August I knew the place well. The four of us drove down from the main house through Chestertown and stayed a couple of days on the Bay.

It was like the set of some movie, a feeling of timelessness about the place, tinged with the sense that something was coming. By the dock was a place called The Crab House. We'd sit outside there in the quiet of the afternoons, gazing at the sky and the water and the boats, drinking wine and eating soft-shell blue crabs. We'd sit there till we were half asleep with the wine and the sun and the breezes, as if on the edge of eternity. I can't recall anything we talked about, there was no need to talk. There were three days of this.

On the drive back, just a few miles out of Rock Hall, Charles suggested we detour to an old churchyard whose historic graves date back to the seventeenth century; more recent ones include that of Tallulah Bankhead. As there were no objections, he made a right turn off Rock Hall Road onto Sandy Bottom Road.

"Why's it called *Sandy Bottom* Road?" Julian wondered.

"Because it has a sandy foundation", I suggested. "Insecure, and appropriate for a road that leads to a graveyard."

We drove along it for a short distance before turning left into the parking lot of the old churchyard of St Paul's Episcopal Church, Kent County. Built in 1713, this was the second building constructed on the site. Its consecrated grounds are planted with a variety of trees and combine the qualities of graveyard and arboretum—fine English and American boxwoods predominate, and there's an outstanding 400-year-old swamp oak, possibly the oldest in Maryland. There are some twenty acres of land in the churchyard, which slopes gently down to a mill-pond that was mirror-smooth on the overcast day we visited. Aside from us there wasn't a soul in sight. The air was still, not even a bird-song to be heard. It was late autumn and the bare trees were deep into the dormancy they paid for rebirth.

"OK, all out!" Charles commanded. "I *know* this place, it's interesting to walk around, so let's see who we can find—*lots* of interesting old folks in *here*!"

The church was closed up, we had no brochure to guide us, so each of us wandered about to find whatever there was to discover.

"Look", Julian exclaimed in surprise. "There's a monument with your surname name on it, Dad, and right alongside it, one with Grandma's maiden name."

It froze me. "You're right! Well-*spotted*!"

A certain Michael Miller, name of a deceased first cousin of mine, had his grave close to the church door. I later found, through the Internet, that he'd sold to the vestry the original plot of eight acres from his Arcadia estate on 6 February 1696 for the equivalent price of 2000 pounds of tobacco, money he later refunded to them. "*Et in Arcadia Ego*" would have looked good on his headstone.

"Here's Daniel Coley, whoever *he* was" Charles observed. "Died 20 October 1729 and sleeps till the resurrection, apparently. Interesting inscription."

We all read it:

Behold and see where now I lie.
As you are now, so once was I;
As I am now, so you must be.
Therefore prepare to follow me.

"You like that, Julian?—the idea of it?" I was thinking he probably hadn't seen the lines before. I'd seen other graves in America and England that bore the same message, or close: "Where you are now, there once were we, and where we are, you too must be."

"No I don't, it's morbid."

"Well, yes … it's morbid, *undeniably* morbid. Striking, though!"

We wandered about not giving a damn and with no idea what we were looking at.

"Look here!" I called to Joan, who was walking close by. "—Hey, Charles! Come over, take a look at this: '1st Lieutenant Samuel Beck, Assistant Surgeon, staff of General John H. Winder, Provost Marshal of Confederate Prisons'."

Charles read the inscription, saying he'd noticed it on a previous visit. General Winder, he told us, had been in charge of Camp Sumter down in Georgia, the place known as Andersonville, one of several prison camps he supervised.

"The place from which Union prisoners emerged like walking skeletons?" I asked.

"Correct—45,000 prisoners penned in there, of whom over 12,000 died of disease and hunger. Though you've got to remember that there was very little food in Georgia in the winter of 1865 and that 33,000 emerged alive, and also that the Union repeatedly refused a prisoner exchange. Sherman supervised rape and pillage clear across Georgia and no-one held *him* to account."

"Forget him, let's find Tallulah. I want to know more about her. Where's *she* laid?" I asked.

"She's across the way, in the newer section."

Julian had never heard of her. "Who was she with a name like that?"

"Star of the silver screen", Charles told him, "—from Alabama. And then in her declining years it was 'as seen on TV'. I once read a book about her. Nice girl till she turned fifteen. And then pretty soon she began to develop and refine those promiscuous ways", he laughed. He thought she probably inherited the self-confidence required to be so outrageous. Her grandfather was a senator from Alabama and her father was Speaker of the House of Representatives before the Second World War. But Julian wasn't paying attention.

"What *kinds* of promiscuous ways?" he wanted to know.

"I don't have all the details, I just read the one book. She called herself 'ambisextrous', 'pure as the driven slush'."

"So she was witty as well as dirty?"

"*Very* witty", Charles went on. "And all of her affairs, and all of her one-night stands, she called them 'momentary impromptus'. Some guy at a party once said to her 'I'd like to sleep with you' and she replied 'And so you shall, you darling little man—today'. Predictably enough she contracted venereal disease, but after the operation she told the surgeon that if he thought this would teach her a lesson he had another think coming. From what I've read she was a good person."

"I've *found* her", I called from about ten yards away. "She's laid over here, under this slab. 'Tallulah Brockman Bankhead' it says. 'January 31, 1902, December 12, 1968'. Doesn't tell you much, does it?"

She'd evidently thought about it and decided to reduce the vanity, fame and display down to nothing, leaving just her three names and a couple of dates. It didn't stand out and it didn't even stand up, just level with the earth.

By now it was time to wander back to the car, and as we strolled through the grounds in that newer section Charles let loose one of those absurd off-handers of his as he surveyed the ground ahead:

"The problem with you people down *here* is you're all *dumb*. And the reason you're all dumb is you're all *dead*."

It was an odd thing to say but not entirely untypical. "Good luck with that", I thought. I suppose he felt on top of the world, but he said it on top of the dead, *to* the dead.

A month later I was back home in Melbourne and decided to call him. He was out and it was Joan who answered. She told me Charles had gone in "for one of those series of tests everyone here seems to have regularly". The PSA test for prostate cancer had come up positive, but the doctor had told him it was perhaps not worth operating—but it was Charles's call. He might die *with* it, way down the track, rather than *from* it. The senior nurse privately cautioned Joan not to allow Charles to have any procedure undertaken. She used terms like "cellular leakage" and "accelerated metastasis"—possible outcomes, she said, of biopsies and cutting procedures. She also mentioned the predictable morbidity: incontinence, diapers, erectile problems, dry orgasms.

Charles couldn't live with doubt and anxiety, he had to have the problem "fixed", that was his word. I spoke with him by telephone a couple of weeks after the operation and he told me about the after-effects. He was optimistic that things would improve. The doctors seemed encouraging. But when I called again a month later it was Joan who answered. New tests revealed that the cancer had spread. It was everywhere.

As the months rolled on it was one dose of morphine per day, then two and finally three. I asked Joan on one of those calls why the hell he didn't just take two doses a day and store up the third for a couple of weeks, then take sixteen. "Get him to do that", I told her. She said he couldn't endure the pain any longer on just two—and what if sixteen didn't kill him? "They'll kill all right", I told her, but then immediately wondered whether they would. His system might throw them back, and he could choke. I apologised for the suggestion, but they'd both thought of it too.

I was glad I wasn't there. By this time, just six months or so since the operation, she was looking after him in a room downstairs as it was too difficult to get him up to the principal bedroom and back down for meals or to carry the meals up to him. He was in enormous pain, the morphine was affecting his personality and he was becoming paranoid. She must be poisoning him, he thought, and he hurled the accusation at her again and again. Then he'd demand that she go upstairs and get his revolver, which he habitually kept loaded (and not with blanks), a reasonable request she declined to fulfil. On one occasion he became so enraged at his situation that he picked up a large vase and hurled it across the room directly at her. She moved and it missed.

Increasingly unmanageable at home, he was transferred to a hospice for the dying where he was turned with insufficient frequency and developed sores all over his body. It was there he died in an agony mitigated by massive doses of morphine a year after our last visit to Rock Hall and the grounds of St Paul's Episcopalian Church in Kent County, Maryland.

I put it down to bad luck, that and the unknowable flow of causes and effects. I miss him. He was fun to be around, had tons of character and a lot of guts.

Index